STRUGGLE & SUCCESS

SUCCESS

STRUGGLE &

Edited by Renée Hollis

TIMELESS WISDOM
True stories that reveal the depths of the human experience

Emotional Inheritance

First published 2020

Emotional Inheritance
An imprint of Exisle Publishing Pty Ltd
PO Box 864, Chatswood, NSW 2057, Australia
226 High Street, Dunedin, 9016, New Zealand
www.exislepublishing.com

A CiP record for this book is available from the National Library of Australia.

ISBN 978-1-925820-08-9

Designed by Nada Backovic
Typeset in 12/18 Sabon Lt Std
Printed in China

This book uses paper sourced under ISO 14001 guidelines from well-managed forests and other controlled sources.

10 9 8 7 6 5 4 3 2 1

'John Darby' (p. 59) is an adapted excerpt from the book *Professor Penguin: Discovery and adventure with penguins* by Lloyd Spencer Davis, published by Random House New Zealand Ltd.

Invictus

Out of the night that covers me,
Black as the pit from pole to pole,
I thank whatever gods may be
For my unconquerable soul.

In the fell clutch of circumstance
I have not winced nor cried aloud.
Under the bludgeonings of chance
My head is bloody, but unbowed.

Beyond this place of wrath and tears
Looms but the Horror of the shade,
And yet the menace of the years
Finds and shall find me unafraid.

It matters not how strait the gate,
How charged with punishments the scroll,
I am the master of my fate,
I am the captain of my soul.

WILLIAM ERNEST HENLEY

CONTENTS

It's the
possibility
of having a
dream come true
that makes life
interesting.

PAULO COELHO

INTRODUCTION

Every day in the news we hear remarkable true stories that demonstrate the resilience of the human spirit. We thought it was time that more of these stories were heard, so we organized an international short story writing competition, which has resulted in the publication of the *Timeless Wisdom* collection of books.

We were overwhelmed by the variety and richness of the hundreds of entries from around the world. Our criteria for final selection were that the stories should reflect a diversity of writing, blend humour and pathos, and balance moments of drama with those of quiet contemplation.

We can all relate to the positive attitude and determination that it takes to overcome challenges in life. Should we embrace the struggle? How can we push through difficult situations? This is the true test of the human spirit. As Paulo Coelho said, 'It's the possibility of having a dream come true that makes life interesting.' The telling moments in this book will enthral you and provide a source of practical inspiration.

From a woman's experience of being married to a compulsive gambler, to a struggling writer's journey of failure and success; from people battling mental illnesses and emerging on the other side, to a 62 year old graduating as a pharmacist — these are stories of unexpected struggle and success that had a lasting impact on the storyteller. Interspersed between the stories are quotes about struggle and success by people as diverse as Martin Luther King Jr., F. Scott Fitzgerald, Oscar Wilde, C.S. Lewis and Demi Lovato. The result is a book that explores all that is best about human nature.

THE RABBIT

Michelanne Forster

At the age of 26 I decided to become an actor. This was not a good idea as I could neither act nor take criticism: a fatal theatrical combination. Nevertheless I wormed my way into the Fortune Theatre in Dunedin, and was immediately cast as a rabbit. I spent the next three months touring Otago and Southland enacting the story of Brer Rabbit to bewildered school children. This was well before New Zealand stories were considered vital for young enquiring minds. After hopping around innumerable country schools singing *Way down yonder in the paw paw patch*, then washing my cotton rabbit ears in a different motel sink every night, I started to become disillusioned.

The company's artistic director took me aside. 'Rome wasn't built in a day,' he said. 'You don't want to get on a main stage too soon.' He smiled in a worrying way. 'Still, perhaps we could cast you in a small part.'

My heart jumped. Out of the rabbit costume at last!

'We're doing *The Lion in Winter* and we need a serf. You'd come on between scenes dressed in a sackcloth, in semi-darkness of course, and move Eleanor of Aquitaine's throne from A to B etcetera.'

He raised his eyebrows as if to ask, was I up to it? Let's just say I became an uber-serf. A serf with a vengeance. I was so determined to have a speaking part before my year as a trainee expired I dragged that fake medieval furniture around like my life depended on it.

When I finally did make it into a main bill production of Roger Hall's play, *Prisoners of Mother England,* I was overjoyed. My hard work had paid off. Then I overheard the director grousing in the theatre bar. 'My god,' he said, slugging his drink. 'Why am I wasting the best years of my life with these *amateurs* in a god-forsaken hole with a boring bloody albatross colony, and a statue of Robbie Burns as its chief cultural monument?'

I vowed to try harder. Unfortunately, the American accent I'd brought with me when immigrating with my family in 1973 hung stubbornly on. Like Eliza Doolittle, I spoke my three hard-won lines carefully, modulating every vowel with a pained expression of intense concentration, but I still sounded like a Hollywood extra on the back lot. The director told me to stop mugging, waggling my hands and pronouncing r's like I had a bush full of burrs in my mouth. Serious doubts began to invade. Maybe I was temperamentally unsuited for the theatrical life? Dictatorial critiques, long spells 'resting' (read: unemployed), crazy hours, poor pay — was this really the career for me? My deliberations were cut short when, one afternoon, the artistic director stormed out. The theatre board quickly hired a replacement. He fired three-quarters of the company, me among them.

I decided to travel north to the Court Theatre in Christchurch in a last-ditch attempt to salvage my less-than-glorious stage career. I set up an audition with a highly regarded director. Terrified would not even begin to describe how I felt as I walked up the narrow wooden stairs to the main rehearsal room. I entered and smiled wanly at the director, who sat waiting for me, bored yet rapacious looking, like a vulture poised to devour. He nodded, and I poured out a heartrendingly overdone speech from *A Streetcar Named Desire*. After two sentences he held up his hand; stop please. He then asked me to reconsider one or two points regarding my character. I gazed at him blankly, nodded and plunged back into the speech once more, a volcano of sloppy emotion. He coughed.

'Perhaps,' he said, in a surprisingly kind voice, 'you can sing?' I toddled off to the piano and warbled through a song, forgetting most of the words. The pianist soldiered on, then mercifully the audition was over. 'You have a very nice face for the stage,' the director said. 'I'll let you know.'

I backed out of the room, almost in tears. I knew then I didn't have, and never would have, the magic a good actor needs. On the train back home to Dunedin I felt raw and hopeless. I'd left a two-year teaching stint to follow a stage-struck dream — and now look at me. I was unemployed, with a student husband, no money and no prospects. All I was, was a failed creative 'wannabe'.

Several weeks later I landed a job at Television New Zealand as a scriptwriter on a children's show called *Play School*. I was over the moon. The idea of a theatrical career suddenly seemed ridiculous. Me an actor? No thank you. Far better to be behind a desk, churning out words for somebody else to say. I quickly adapted to the discipline of writing and editing the mountain of scripts that came pouring through our office from the BBC. Within two years I was training to be a television studio and film director in the children's and young person's department. After a nearly a decade, I was fired again. Well, actually I was made redundant, when our two-channel television service became an SOE, or state-owned enterprise. This time, however, I didn't panic. I had a solid set of skills and two young children. I decided to work freelance as a writer.

In 1991 the same Christchurch theatre director I'd once auditioned for now asked me to sit in on rehearsals for a new play I had written called *Daughters of Heaven*. Little did I know that this play, based on a historical matricide, would become a New Zealand staple. To this day, the play is studied and performed by high school students around the country and has had numerous professional productions.

I'm 65 now, with a long career in the creative arts. My CV declares I am an author, a playwright, a scriptwriter, a dramaturg and a teacher. It doesn't say I am a rabbit. However, inside I know I was a rabbit once, one who accidentally fell down the hole into her professional life. The memories of those cotton ears keep me humble. Whenever I see one of my stage productions, I'm filled with admiration for the actors who bring my words to life with their unique skill and passion. Wherever I sell a story, or hold a book I've published, I think what a joy it is to be able to express myself this way. And to get paid to do it! Yes, talent was needed, and perseverance, but there was also an element of plain dumb luck. I was one of the lucky ones. That desire to create bloomed inside me once, and it still keeps me going.

However long the night, the dawn **will** break.

AFRICAN PROVERB

DIFFERENT SONGSHEETS, DIFFERENT TUNES

Garrick Batten

Farmers certainly can't control the weather. That year, a giant rain umbrella was over the farm — a summer rain shadow persisting for weeks. It followed thunderstorms ruining one lot of hay, and then strong, dry, oven-whoof winds crisping pastures. As the radio guys kept telling us, great weather for tourists and schoolkids on holiday, but our animal feed was disappearing as fast as kids spent their pocket money.

I was sick of the scent of dust. And the wind started to sound evil — a goblin puffed hot gale-force gusts some days. Empty blue skies were blazing, blowtorching, repetitively boring. Other 'b' words on my lips. We faced a serious drought. At least wet sheep didn't hold up the shearers. Wool was important at 70 per cent of our income in the first couple of years. Then the auction price dropped 15 per cent by the end of the 1980s, and was much more significant to our bottom line now.

I faced uncertainty that any drought brings. Should we reduce stock numbers or buy in more feed? Should we sell stock or send some away for grazing? When would it rain? Would there be enough rain if it did? Would it ever rain? I anxiously watched stock condition and pastures. Some lambs were slipping back, but the freezing works were flat out killing, and getting more space was difficult. I made some plans with trigger dates for action to reduce stock. One way or another, any decision would cost us money and blow the budget.

No pocket money for our kids. And Christmas coming up. Their Rolling Stones CDs seemed a chorus for our lives, with *You can't always get what you want* and *I can't get no satisfaction*.

Weather is one of the undeniable facts farmers have to learn to live with. Lambing date is set when rams go out, months before any possible summer drought. Although we expected changes, each year was different, and unknown in advance. Rarely exactly the right weather — perhaps one of the reasons for farmers' reputation for grumbling. At the same time, this constant challenge was always a talk topic with others. And also with oneself, one we collectively anticipated each day, and at night as we lay awake planning how and where to feed stock. But wisdom now taught we could always have faith in nature that things would eventually come right.

Each morning I looked for clouds, and in the afternoons I watched towering, billowing thunderheads in fantastic shapes form over the back mountains. The burning royal blue of the sky, fading to a lighter blue on the hill edges, refused to turn grey and black as each day wore on. Never any rain in the sky. The Stones track *Fool to cry* was appropriate.

❁

It was disturbing when the bank manager called for a meeting to revise the budget and explore future options. We dressed in our best clothes. Ruth redid her nails, suggested I wore a tie, and gathered our budgets and plans. We practised confident, smiling faces on the drive to town. As she checked her make-up in the mirror Ruth told me she had been secretly dreading this meeting. She probably better understood our financial position; her woman's intuition knew we were stretched too far by empty sky. Was the heat suffocating our future? Our farming dream turning into a real nightmare?

The car CD drive played more Stones with *Doom and gloom*, but I turned it off when they started on *It's all over now*.

A new bank manager. His first manager's job. A young man, clearly on the way up the ladder, sent to the province to straighten out some slack management creeping in. With clear head office instructions, and not seeming to understand that banks need clients for their business, or that farming was not like his town background and experience. His dark, cold-looking eyes carried no compassion as they lasered back at us. Ruth tried to small-talk him using her charm that had snared me all those years ago. But he was single, so no common children's tales to share, didn't play any sport, and hadn't even used the weekends to explore the district. In fact, it also seemed his bosses expected him to learn about farming on the job without understanding anything about it. Or maybe wanting us to teach him.

He was quickly typing on the newly installed computer as we discussed various scenarios. All beyond me. I could only finger the cherrywood pipe in my pocket, confused and frustrated. Everything was on the line: our business, our life, our home and our future. We had renewed pastures with new varieties. The bank had lent us money for more fertilizer and fencing two years ago and that took time to produce results. Could I blame the bank for funding us into this hole? No, I couldn't blame it, so it shouldn't be able to blame us for this drought. We knew things would eventually come right. It just needed time, continuing agreed plans, and some rain. He could not, or would not, understand.

After an hour and a half of increasing tension, he suggested we should go away and think about how we could help him satisfy his boss within their rules and policies. We scheduled another meeting in a week, and left to pick up some groceries, dog biscuits, new season's apples, and a part for the tractor on the way out of town. And he wouldn't even understand why we did that then.

We drove home in silence, minds whirling, my pipe smoke filling the car with burning resentment at barking-mad bank bureaucracy. We were doing the absolute best we could, and it was never going to be an easy farm. I was tempted to turn around and go back and give him some reality. Individual farms could not fit into one flickering spreadsheet. Farm management needs long-term solutions to short-term problems. A farming business is about a jigsaw of land, labour and capital. We had the farm, and used our skills and long hours to work with nature to manage it. The bank had to come to the party too with some money — that was their business. But they had us vice-gripped, and I couldn't find the release lever.

Ruth could always read my feelings, so beside me in the passenger seat she knew how I'd be thinking and how I might react. Straight up the hill. Perhaps there were other ways, she suggested, like getting this new townie manager out to the farm, taking him to our back paddock hill and explaining what we had done and would do. No problem to arrange a fine day.

She turned on the radio for some music to soothe me. Split Enz singing *My mistake*. She switched off, but at least it wasn't their *Poor boy*.

After half an hour the soft drumming of ute tyres changed to other musical noises of clattering stones as we left the sealed road. Later we started to splash through puddles. The closer to home we got, the more the sky closed in, weeping at our predicament.

The teasing drizzle had stopped by the time we got home, but a soft, steady, drought-breaking rain fell all night and the next day, the gentle scuffing sound on the iron roof like Charlie Watts' brushes on the snare. The gurgling downpipe was playing the melody and was all the music we needed to hear now. Bliss to doze through the night to that lullaby. Then a big storm next day, bringing high winds, sodden rain, flooded creeks and damaged floodgates. We didn't lose any stock, even though it was now spread into wrong paddocks and the neighbour's.

City folk rarely understand the delights and disasters of weather. I got the kids to play *Start me up* as I pranced around like Mick Jagger. Next morning, I stood in the veranda sun with a promising smell of soaking soil and grass wafting off steaming paddocks. The girls picked mushrooms over the following week. I had to start fixing fences and clearing up blown-over trees.

The scheduled bank meeting had a completely different tone and result. While the manager could still not appreciate what 3 inches of rain could do for grass growth, my budgets and his spreadsheets now had a green, not red, tinge. I could turn green grass into prime stock, and he could turn those into spreadsheet figures to show his boss how he'd sorted this particular customer. Photos of physical damage to their security opened a different purse for repairs too, so we won a bit more. I'm not sure our relationship with the bank manager was fully repaired, but he could now have the Stones tune *I can't get no satisfaction* to himself. And we could hum along to *Time is on my side* as we watched grass grow.

There are
better starters
than me but
I'm a **strong**
finisher.

USAIN BOLT

ANSTOCK THE KING

Elizabeth Sinclair

Wakened by the radio — the biannual teachers' strike — feet land softly on the silk rug.

The fragrance wafts — coffee brewing.

Change the station — Handel's *Zadok the Priest*.

Suddenly I think of him — Mr Anstock.

Anstock, the King.

❧

Life was different back then, in the days of growing.

'Can I join the Brownies?'

'How much does it cost?'

'Can I go to Sunday school with Glenda?'

'Ask yer faither.'

'Can I join the library?'

'If you lose any books, I'm not paying for them.'

The 1960s were beckoning and my eight-year-old self was going through a 'joining' phase that lasted for a few years.

We had moved away from the coalfield, the miners' housing where I had been born, and were transplanted into a freshly planned town.

But Mum was lost. She had no personal experience of the options I paraded before her. She didn't prevent me from joining anything as long as it didn't involve a significant financial outlay, and no investment of her time. *Valium* was her friend. The pills made hobbies redundant.

But I wasn't carrying around the burden of her history, nor those of a long line of women who had handled deprivation. In this new place, I was no longer thought of as the progeny of the pit, the men with coal-ingrained skin and eyes seemingly startled by daylight. These images had been wiped away along with the grime on the journey south, on the moving truck.

Then fate lent a hand in the shape of a newly built, freshly painted school and an ever-so-slightly eccentric headmaster, Mr Anstock, an ex-air force pilot. He smoked a pipe, had floppy hair, tossed back from time to time. He wore tweeds. He just reeked of class.

At school assembly every morning he invariably played a piece of classical music to get us going. He favoured the Romantic composers, particularly Tchaikovsky. The *1812* still makes me think I should be running around doing something heroic.

'Can we get a Tchaikovsky record?'

'What the hell are you talking about?'

Pupils were streamed, with bright young things like me in the A stream. Reading and talking up a storm were my strengths — arithmetic, not so much. I loved quizzes. I knew about European capital cities and that van Gogh only sold one painting in his lifetime. I was a trivia sponge.

'Can we get a set of encyclopaedias?'

'D'you think we're the royal bloody family?'

To pit us against each other in school competitions and sports events, Mr Anstock divided us into four school houses named after people he saw as heroic and inspirational. Bader House was named for Douglas Bader, World War II pilot and well-known double amputee. Hillary House honoured Edmund Hillary, the first man to reach the summit of Mount Everest. Dr Albert Schweitzer was a missionary doctor and theologian who worked in what was known as the 'dark African continent'. I had an image of myself as the missionary type and really wanted to be in Schweitzer House but alas, it was not to be.

You have to laugh at the comic antics of the universe when a girl from the coalfield had go home to tell her parents she had been allocated to Churchill House. Churchill! Aristocrat, reputed hater of miners, and not so keen on votes for women. If my soul had been put on Earth to learn the meaning of irony, we should have called the lesson over right there. But in reality, I could hardly confess to our uber-patriotic headmaster how my family felt about Winston and his historical antipathy to my people. An appeal for a transfer was not on — I was pigeonholed. The house colour was a good fit.

'I need a yellow T-shirt for school.'

'What next?'

Another plank in our leader's mission to civilize the kids in his charge involved animals. He had a pet fox, a vixen actually, kept in a run on the school grounds. Later, a pet sheep arrived. I remember them being kept far apart. These school animals represented my only consistent childhood contact with the four-legged ones.

'Can I have a dog?'

'No, you're scared of dogs.'

'I'm not.'

'Yes, you are!'

That settled that. No dog for me.

I remember him, Anstock, Professor Higgins to our Eliza Doolittles, and he was preternaturally dedicated to moulding and nurturing young minds. He did so softly, the smoke from his pipe drifting upwards. He set out a pallet of thoughts and concepts unlikely to be offered at home. They were not forced on us, just gently waved with enough repetition to give them the stickiness ideas need to permanently influence.

He favoured good penmanship as evidence of an educated mind. He was going to create true renaissance scholars, never mind the cost of the special nibs required for our fountain pens.

'I need a pen with an italic nib for school.'

'Don't they supply those?'

'No.'

'How much?'

They say after seven years, every cell in the human body has been replenished. This meant the eight-year-old me must have had very few cells left over from being birthed in the coalfield. I was now an A-stream, italic-writing, classical music-listening, Brownie-attending Churchillian, with access to wild animals. Reinvented.

The first schoolfriend I remember was Janet, who lived a few doors away. She was horse crazy and took riding lessons on Saturday mornings. At first, we would pretend to canter back from school. Those were the days when eight year olds could ride their imaginary ponies home alone, along a footpath through trees useful for tethering our rides.

'Can I get riding lessons?'

'Ask yer faither.'

'Dad, can I get riding lessons?'

'No, it's too expensive.'

Clearly, I'd hit some kind of barrier — horse riding. Not for the likes of us. Mr Anstock could only do so much.

My friendship with Janet lasted only until she found a couple of sister equestrians, and I didn't get into the gang. I couldn't contribute to the chatter about tack, jumps and how many hands-high a colt was but, with what became a lifelong capacity for trivia, I still remember a hand is equal to 4 inches. Take that pony girl!

With the way the dice is thrown in the game, home for the eight-year-old me could have been the single determinant of how things would go in my life. How would it have been without Anstock the King?

Home.

On weekends we would go to a local workmen's club. There, my parents could enjoy music and dancing and, because they sold food, kids were allowed on the premises — bonus for them, no babysitting problems.

In the way a drinking binge has of begetting the need for more alcohol, many Saturday nights we would bundle into a fleet of taxis after the club closed and go back to our house. I would drag myself off to bed and they would party on. Sometimes they'd insist I perform my signature song, *Danny boy,* before I retired for the night. My rendering was obviously so sweet, Mum would start to cry and through her sobs tell everyone this was her father's favourite. Let's face it, those kinds of experiences leave a mark.

Of course, one of the downsides of that lifestyle was not being able to talk about my weekends with school mates. They were going for trips to parks and places of interest. They were having dinner with their extended family. They were learning to play the cello. I was keeping company with drinkers in a glorified bar. And believe me, having an unusual knowledge of whisky brands didn't cut it with the cool kids.

I stayed quiet about my real weekend exploits until I developed a rich imaginary life. In other words, I got comfy with lying.

'I had a picnic with all the family on Sunday.'

'Mum and Dad are going to take me to the circus.'

'Dad's bought a new car so we can drive out into the country.'

❈

All these years later I am ready for the day for which Anstock had helped prepare me. I fill the travel mug, find the car keys, pick up the soft red briefcase, my presentation is ready on the laptop. People are waiting for me — *for me*.

Thank you, Sir. We were only ever allowed to call you 'Sir,' like a king.

I'm so sorry I didn't ever take the chance to say it personally. But if it is any consolation, whenever I hear *Zadok the Priest*, I substitute the words 'Anstock the King'.

You don't
have to see the
whole staircase,
just take the
first step.

MARTIN LUTHER KING JR.

MY WRITING LIFE

Shane Joseph

I have been drawn to writing ever since I was a child, a rather sickly child who seemed to attract every illness that blew in the wind back in my native Sri Lanka: *filariasis*, pneumonia, chicken pox, mumps, measles. They even took out my infected adenoids and tonsils at one point and condemned me to a lifetime of allergies, colds and flu. I spent a lot of time away from school and read copiously during those periods, a prerequisite to writing, I was later to discover.

It helped that I had an uncle who worked in a bookshop and brought me the latest releases to 'read and return'. Given that the books had to be in sellable condition when I finished reading them, I had to use them with extreme respect or lose the privilege. So I would wrap them in brown paper covers and refrain from dog-earing the pages, and I left food and liquids out of reach when I read.

I was fascinated by the writer's ability to transport the reader to worlds far away. While my world was a hot and steamy tropical one with the sounds of dogs barking, chickens clucking and vendors shouting on the street, these worlds were the Wild West, Revolutionary France, Victorian England, Tsarist Russia, anywhere I chose to go from the sickly confines of my room. I lived vicariously through Richmal Crompton's impish William, and Franklin W.

Dixon's *Hardy Boys* (later in life I discovered to my dismay that Dixon was a conglomerate of many writers writing to a formula). As I grew older, I snuck into my dad's Ian Fleming collection, much against his admonishments, given the amount of sex that James Bond indulged in. Sex? Bond is pretty tame compared to the more popular fare available today. I matured into the novels of Graham Greene and marvelled at his ability to stir up guilt in humans; and in Hemingway's desire to face death all the time, not just in the afternoon; and in Steinbeck's biblical allegories.

I began writing when I was seventeen, determined to become like one of my heroes of the pen, dreaming of sending manuscripts into the world that would become bestsellers and make me a reclusive millionaire like Salinger, so that I could hide out on some remote island and submit more manuscripts and continue to dazzle the world with my brilliance until I was invited to a cold capital in Europe to accept the Nobel Prize. And I would *refuse* that honour, making me an even more enigmatic figure; you could see that Jean-Paul Sartre and Boris Pasternak had influenced me greatly. I wrote stories about underprivileged kids, adults in marital conflicts, and adolescent boys having a Holden Caulfield moment. I was fortunate to come under the influence of my first mentor, James Goonewardene, a published novelist in Sri Lanka, who read my work and told me quite bluntly that I knew nothing about underprivileged kids because I did not live like them, that I was too young to understand grown-ups and their marital challenges, but that my adolescent stories had, well … promise.

So I renewed my efforts, churning out YA stories. One was finally published at the end of that first year, and at the age of seventeen I became a published author. Of course, I never published anything for the next seven years. I was preoccupied with studies and with earning money in a country where the inflation rate was running upwards of 50 per cent, a country plunging steadily into civil war. Then, unexpectedly, I turned out a masterpiece (at least, in my mind): I wrote a story which was an exposé on child prostitution in the tourist industry. I felt like Solzhenitsyn exposing the ills of Stalinism. The national radio station accepted my story for its weekly literary program and then rejected it at the last minute on the grounds that 'it would not be good for tourism'. I felt elevated to literary sainthood: a banned story! But I was also crushed because my voice had been silenced, and at the age of 24 that was a cruel experience.

❀

I spent the next twenty years suppressing the urge to write, focusing instead on raising a family, emigrating to the West, and building a business career. But just as you can't keep a good story down, you can't keep a raging torrent dammed up forever. About seventeen years ago the dam burst, and out poured the stories that had accumulated like flotsam over the years. I was finally able to write with authority on underprivileged people because I had come to Canada as an immigrant; I wrote about adult marital situations because I'd had plenty of those myself; and I had not lost my hold on my inner Holden Caulfield — he was alive and well, and *bolder*. I wish my old mentor James Goonewardene was still alive, but he had long since shuffled off this mortal coil.

I discovered that being a 21st century author was a different experience to that of my heroes of the previous century, who were now all dead. Writing was a democracy and not an aristocracy any more. Technology had influenced everything, including writing. I discovered that more than the quality of the content, writing was about branding and franchising, about endorsement and winning awards. The 1 per cent theory holds very true in literature today, even the '1 per cent of the 1 per cent' that is now being talked about. And the middle years I had spent in accumulating flotsam had been squandered by not building my 'platform'.

Ever the optimist, I began to build this amorphous platform with ageing muscles. I built a website, reviewed books and blogged, and gave away a lot of free content. I self-published, then had my work accepted by trade publishers. I was published anywhere anyone was willing to publish my work. Soon I had several novels and collections of short stories in print. Even my banned exposé on child prostitution was finally published — after 30 years, and merited mention on the Canadian Broadcasting Corporation. The irony: rejected by one broadcaster and celebrated by another!

I learnt the tools of publishing, used technology to my advantage, and became a trade publisher myself. I derive tremendous satisfaction in being able to help other authors realize their own work in published form. I look back on the last seventeen years and realize that, although I might not have washed up on that remote island with millions of dollars, I am on some kind of an island surrounded by my stories.

In the course of my writing odyssey I have faced rejection, the writer's badge of honour. But I do not get crushed by it any more. I have had my manuscripts lost by publishers; I have had curt notes sent to me saying that I was writing 'crap'; I have endured cold silences from the other side; I have fired literary agents and publishers for inaction, and have been fired in turn; I have also speed-dated with agents and publishers and had some productive experiences. But through it all, I have held on to my voice, for that is all a writer has. Once, when I was asked to change the locales in my novel *The Ulysses Man* from Sri Lanka and Canada to India and the United States because there were larger book-buying markets in the latter countries, I refused and bowed out of a potential book deal. I ended up poorer in the pocketbook but my soul felt good!

Writing has helped me heal. Over the course of a life we develop neuroses, hurts and grievances. The world is against you as you 'suffer the slings and arrows of outrageous fortune'. Writing helps resolve these ills and let go. When pressed, I create horrible characters with dislikable traits and kill them off — a form of catharsis. It's safer than knocking off real people.

How many stories does a writer have in them? I think the answer is 'unlimited'. Once you finish writing the stories that are close to your life, you reach out to other lands and times. With the research material available at our fingertips today via the internet, it is possible to marry content with imagination and dream up other worlds. My 2009 novel, *After the Flood*, takes place in the year 2047, my version of it. I just completed writing a trilogy set in the 1790s, based on the life of an adventurous ancestor, a saga that moves from France to South Africa to the Indian subcontinent. It has taken me seven years to complete the trilogy and I travelled to all three locations for my research. I am not sure whether the trilogy will ever see the light of day as a published work, but its writing journey was soul-enriching.

And what of the future? I don't fret, and trust my imagination instead. For surely, when the next story is ready to be born, the muse will reappear.

Your mind and
attitudes create either
barriers or bridges to
good outcomes.

AL SIEBERT

BIBI

Eugen Bacon

She was a different kind of girl.

She was the fastest in the village, and the prettiest. Bibi had the neck of an ostrich and the lashes of a leopard. She could run miles, balancing a pot full of water from the lake without holding it. Not only was she the prettiest girl in the village but the brightest. Brighter than her brothers. By the time she could walk, she could charm the meat of a chicken or a goat, even tongues or gizzards, from her brothers' mouths. Her brothers Alexi and Melkiadi never caught up with Bibi.

Bibi was a pioneer. Unable to stay indifferent, she contradicted the world of riddles and the mastery of men. She was the first woman in her family to be educated — girls didn't go to school those days. They learnt how to make good wives.

But Christianity came to native lands. It suffocated the gods of the thorn tree and the Kilimanjaro. Catholics at the mission house baptized Bibi's mother and the other children's mothers, before turning to the children and their would-be spouses because missionaries travelled like the waters of the Nile. They reached the township of Musoma where the boy Aloyse, who would grow up and one day marry Bibi, was first named Matthew, like the name in the Bible. But nobody in his village could say it right and the name became Matthayo, then Mateo and finally Matoyo, which stuck.

From when she was little, Bibi watched the German sister from a distance, as she taught village boys to read and write under the big mango tree. But little Bibi didn't just watch. She sat at Sister's feet, and no beating — her mother was nimble with a stick — could take the child away from Sister's feet, or the learning. Finally, Sister saw and understood the stars trapped inside Bibi. So she talked the child's father into sending Bibi to a real school far out in the outskirts of the village, in a place called Murutunguru.

Bibi ran miles barefoot to and from primary school each day, and later became the first woman from the village to become a teacher. But despite being a *msomi*, the traditional name for one who was educated, Bibi stayed close to culture and men fell over themselves for her hand in marriage.

But she had her eye on Aloyse, the late Atanasi Musiba's son.

Atanasi Musiba was a friend of Bibi's father. Atanasi came all the way from the town of Musoma to the village to beg Bibi's hand for one of his six sons: Ludovick, Tarasizi, Aloyse, Christopher, Fortunatus or Francis. To everyone's surprise, and her mother's disapproval because it was flouting tradition, Bibi's father let her choose. Nobody had let Bibi's mother choose; a wedding had been arranged, a man was brought and she married him. But Bibi got to see her groom. She put a finger on his face in the picture Atanasi brought along and picked him, way before her wedding day.

Bibi's mother relented. The young man Aloyse had an honest face and eyes that looked directly at you. A thing about him encouraged you to trust him. He was also a *msomi*, educated like Bibi. He travelled the world and presented at conferences overseas.

He would take her to see many places, lands bigger than the village, the towns of Mwanza, Musoma or even the city of Dar-es-Salaam. Bibi's mother understood that the school in Murutunguru had done its work. Bibi wanted to see the world.

❀

The wedding of Bibi and Aloyse was talk of the village for days and days, before and afterwards. As the ceremony drew closer, hour upon hour, anticipation climbed. Suddenly, that dawn, song erupted. The moment everyone was waiting for had arrived.

Dancers swished sisal skirts here, beaded shoulders there. And the feet! Caked with red dust, their toes tapped on the earth in sync to the *ndombolo* drum. The dancers' heels made loops in the air, sprayed soil with each thump of the ground.

But although Bibi's arms shone with copper and gold trinkets, she was not coated with animal fat or wearing a sisal skirt. Bibi's ivory gown was a gift from the mission, a tiered outfit whose hems fell aground and sprawled like a snow-kissed grassland. She looked like a queen in it. Aloyse, he wore a black suit and a tie. No villager had ever seen anything more culturally distant than that.

Unsure how to navigate their feet inside floral dresses longer than the 'Sunday bests' they wore once a week to and from church, little girls tottered along with bracelets of purple and white Jacaranda blossoms.

Aloyse had shipped in crates and crates of white man's beer called Safari. It came in brown bottles, not a calabash. That beer was not made for sharing: every person drank from their own bottle. People still drank it, even though it tasted like cow urine — given as medicine in finger-tip drops to babies who had the type of belly wind that pushed out bad stool and a squeal.

Villagers cheered when it was time to cut the big white cake decorated with flowers, a thing of awe that the sisters from Murutunguru had baked. After the feasting and dancing, people watched in amusement as Aloyse carried Bibi over his shoulder. He put her in a car, his car.

When he took Bibi away, amusement turned to fear for the children, as Aloyse's blue car bellowed like the crocodile that nearly took a child but didn't because villagers cornered it and beat it with sticks. The crocodile's sound saved the child because the beast opened its mouth to bellow. So Bibi's wedding, the talk of the town, ended with a car's roar, but was the start of a happily ever.

This is the story of my mother, Bibi, who was a different kind of girl, one who shaped her own destiny. It is a story of struggle and success that was the beginning of me and my own adventure into the world. I am African Australian and now live in Melbourne.

Wings are not
only for birds;
they are also for
minds. Human
potential stops
at some point
somewhere
beyond infinity.

TOLLER CRANSTON

FREEDOM TO READ

Jane Arnold

When I regret all the things I haven't done to make the world a better place, I remind myself that I have taught adults to read. In turn, they have taught me that learning to read leads them to freedom.

When I realized that the remedial writing students in my community college classes couldn't write because they couldn't read, I enrolled in a specialized training program to teach dyslexics to read. The Orton-Gillingham method is the foundation for nearly all the multi-sensory phonics reading programs in the country. Once trained, I had no problem finding functionally illiterate adults willing to commit to a three-day-a-week tutoring schedule so they could to learn to read.

My first student, Lena, was a 24-year-old community college student from a Portuguese farming family, whose members were nearly all dyslexic and illiterate. Her high school program had operated on the premise that 'these kids will never be smart enough to go to college anyway' and didn't put much emphasis on academics. Lena was smart enough to make it through high school by laboriously deciphering the first and last sentences of a piece of writing and guessing what ought to come in between. On the computerized, untimed, multiple choice reading placement test at the college, she'd spent an hour and a half instead of the more usual 20 minutes and convinced the computer that she didn't need a reading class. Then she hit an accounting textbook. Intelligent guesses didn't work any more. She came to me, and we met three times a week for a year so I could tutor her in reading.

One day in the middle of a lesson, Lena stopped and looked at me. 'I need to get the name of that program you're doing,' she said. 'I think if my brother could learn to read, he'd feel a lot better about himself. I know I feel so much better now that I can read.'

David was a 29-year-old technician in a specialized medical imaging field. He drove to my house through Boston traffic two nights a week and on Sunday morning so I could tutor him. His willingness to drive from Jamaica Plain to Arlington during Boston rush hour testified to his determination. He was the first illiterate dyslexic I met who was already emotionally a reader. Many people who struggle with reading avoid written texts, depending on TV or other aural means for information. But David collected books he fully intended to read — someday.

David came to me with books he'd bought because he wanted to read them. He wanted to read *The DaVinci Code* because everyone else at work had read it. He wanted to read Greek myths. He had managed to get into and graduate from his technical program because he'd gone to the department at a hospital and said, 'I need to work here. I'll do anything.' He learnt by seeing, by doing, and after a year he learnt enough to pass the certification program.

Among the books David chose to read was Ron Davis' controversial *The Gift of Dyslexia*. He chose it, he said, because no one had ever before told him he had a gift: 'There was always just something wrong with me that had to be fixed.'

Davis writes that dyslexics can mentally manipulate images in three dimensions. 'Can you do that?' I asked David.

'Sure,' he answered. 'It's easy.'

I just stared. 'David,' I said, 'not only is it not easy, I don't even know what he's talking about. That must be why you're such a good imaging technician. When I see an X-ray, I say, "Yeah, uh, uh-huh, uh-huh" and all those black-and-white squiggles don't mean a thing. When you look at something like that, it's in 3D.'

The last time I saw David, he told me about an offer he'd received from a company marketing a new electronic imaging technology. They wanted to hire him to travel to hospitals and teach other technicians about the new device. He was intrigued, but said he'd miss his patients.

'If you take this offer,' I said, 'and you decide you don't like it, can you go back to your current job?'

'Oh sure,' he said, 'no problem.'

Then he said, 'Before we began working together, before I learnt to read, if I'd received an offer like this, I would have assumed I couldn't possibly do it, and I never would have considered it. But now I can read.'

Three years later, David taught two seminars at the national conference of the professional society in his specialized area. He's listed as a co-author for papers whose titles I can't even understand.

Like Lena, Rosa was a remedial reading student in a community college class who came from an extended dyslexic family. Like David, she was a reading illiterate. She adored James Patterson. When she read the books aloud for lessons, it was obvious that, although she followed the main plot and had the characters clearly in her mind, she wanted to glaze over about a third of the material that she couldn't decode or understand. (I wouldn't let her — she had to decode what she could, and we worked on vocabulary.) Skimming and skipping in a James Patterson novel isn't a problem. It's a major problem when reading a textbook on whose content the reader will be tested.

We worked together three times a week in the spring semester, her first. In June, Rosa emailed me to ask when we could begin tutoring again. I was teaching a summer school class, and I told her that if she could get to college two days a week for tutoring, I'd meet her on the third day at the town library near her house. She had no car, and the local buses ran every three hours, but she made it to the college two days a week. When I later told her she was a role model for struggling students, she looked at me blankly. 'Why?' she said.

'Because you work so hard and don't give up,' I said.

She shrugged. 'I knew I wasn't going to make it through college reading the way I did.'

Rosa was myopic and had health problems. She occasionally referred to her family — a cousin in prison who was illiterate in both English and his first language, Spanish, or her six-year-old nephew who didn't know the alphabet and whose father said, 'Hey, I can't read, so what? I'm just fine.' When occasionally I asked her if she had learnt a common concept she would comment, 'Of course not. I grew up in the Bronx.' (She was in her mid thirties when we met.) She'd never been out of New York State. When I went to the public library, I could be fairly sure of finding Rosa there at the computers. She had no computer at home.

Rosa claimed to hate history, but she watched both the Discovery and the History channels regularly, and delighted in making connections between the reading and information she remembered from television. She made even more connections when I brought in visuals to aid the reading (maps, photos, pictures of gargoyles).

One day I received an email from Rosa with the subject line 'Thanks'.

> *I just got a test back and there were easy questions. I did what you said to do from govt class and I got 17 out of a possible 21. So THANK YOU very much.*

We worked together for two and a half years. Two semesters later, Rosa took four heavy-duty academic courses, including my literature course in classic world scripture, a sophomore level class. She made the Dean's List that semester. I think I told everyone on campus, I was so proud of her. A year later, she was a college graduate. When her son was born, the first thing she said to him was, 'You're going to college.'

The Irish statesman Edmund Burke said, 'No one makes a greater mistake than he who did nothing because he could only do a little.' A few more adults who can read, and two, at least, who have graduated from college, seems little compared to the world's problems. But I am grateful for the privilege of having worked with these extraordinary people. When another of my students, Linda, was in her thirties, she was still being told, 'You're not very good at school, dear, but you're a lovely mother' (translation: you're just not very smart). Free now from embarrassment and shame, she can say, 'I have a Bachelor degree in psychology. I'm smart. And my kids are, too.'

If there is no struggle, there is no progress.

FREDERICK DOUGLASS

JOHN DARBY

Lloyd Spencer Davis

If anyone could ever be excused, by dint of their circumstances, for feeling hard done by, it is John Darby. Born in Yorkshire, England, on 28 May 1936, the very next day he was placed in the care of one of England's societies that provided homes for waifs and strays.

By the time he left school at age fourteen, after what had been up to that point a life of 'fairly miserable years', John had lived in seven different orphanages. There had been a briefly positive but ultimately heart-wrenching period of a few months in the home of prospective adoptive parents as part of a trial adoption. This was when Britain was being bombed, and he would be herded into air-raid shelters, the sounds of sirens ringing in his ears, the gas mask making him claustrophobic. Most nights there were blackouts, which meant he could watch the searchlights looking for planes. But during this period, as only a seven year old, he lost an eye in a terrible accident. Long periods in hospital, frightful pain, and several bouts of surgery followed and then five months after the accident, he was sent back to an orphanage.

Despite all these adversities, however, the young John Darby was anything but cowed. His many attempts at running away from the orphanages had the benefit of enabling him to discover a love of the natural history of the English countryside: 'Running away was a balancing act between the punishment I would receive when I was caught and returned to the orphanage versus the peace and freedom I would have with the natural history and beauty of the countryside I loved so much.' And although he may not have loved his enforced places of residence, he did love school, particularly anything to do with science.

He left school at fourteen, however, to work as a farmhand. This meant he didn't have to continue living in an orphanage and it would also give him the resources to find his mother. But by the age of sixteen, his search fruitless, he came to the realization that she must not want to be found and so he decided to seek a new life.

That was when he had his first lucky break. A question to a speaker at a Young Farmers' Club meeting led to him going to New Zealand at seventeen to work as a farmhand at Lincoln College. A wonderful new life beckoned, one in which no one knew of his background — a background of which, in the class-dominated English society, he had been made to feel so ashamed. Immediately he set about enhancing his education by enrolling at the Christchurch Polytechnic.

Yet for all the promise New Zealand held for John, it also contained its share of hurdles. After eighteen months, he contracted polio and spent nearly a year in hospital in Auckland without family or friends. Scarcely able to move, he was lonely and scared. Farming, rather cruelly, had been taken off his agenda.

After recovering, he completed his diploma in agriculture and got a job as a technician working in a team researching facial eczema in livestock; he was in 'science heaven', but eventually resigned so that he could study for a degree in zoology at the University of Canterbury. His first year did not go well, but then he got his second lucky break in a life that, thus far, had overwhelmingly ladled out luck of another kind: he was appointed as a technician in the Department of Zoology, with the intention of allowing him to continue his studies part-time. It was there that he was asked to assist with the research of senior lecturer and well-known penguin biologist Bernard Stonehouse, which was how — ten years after coming to New Zealand — he found himself a member of a University of Canterbury Antarctic research team counting Emperor penguins at Cape Crozier.

If John had any doubts about where his future might lie, his fate was sealed that day at Cape Crozier. When the helicopter landed Bernard and John there, one of the Americans who greeted them was Bill Sladen, who in his own way was every bit as famous and influential as Bernard when it came to being a penguin biologist. So there was John in the Antarctic, accompanied by the two fathers of modern penguin biology and surrounded by 'one of the most stunning animals' he had ever encountered. It seemed he had found his family at last.

John would go on to spend three summers assisting with studies of Adelie penguins and skuas at Cape Bird, where he slept in the same bunk I would eventually use, and carved his name into the bottom of the bunk above, so that it was there for me to read a decade later. He would move to Dunedin to become assistant director of the Otago Museum while devoting almost all his free time to the study and conservation of the Yellow-eyed penguins breeding on the Otago Peninsula and beyond. He was instrumental in the establishment of protected areas for the penguins at a time when habitat destruction was threatening their very survival. He set up a banding program and a database of nest records that would extend back over 25 years of research, allowing both himself and the many students with whom he has been associated to analyse the factors affecting penguin breeding success in ways that other studies can only dream about.

Together, John and I would organize the first international conference on penguins, and we have remained fast friends ever since. Eventually, John would complete his degree; persistent to a fault. And that is actually the quality I most admire in John: he is determinedly persistent in the very best of ways. He does not give up, no matter what difficulties or challenges lie before him. Instead, he embraces them and, ultimately, he triumphs.

❈

In 1986, while in England on sabbatical leave from the museum, John once again tried to track down his mother. His detective work took him to a village in Leicester called Barrow upon Soar, where the graveyard revealed a cluster of Darbys but none with his mother's name. As John went to enter the local church, a vicar, on his way out, asked if he could help. John explained that he was looking for his mother and gave the vicar the only name he had to go on. 'Oh,' the vicar said, 'she never married and is in Burton

Hall.' Five minutes later, John was at Burton Hall, an old people's home just down the road, being ushered into a room to meet a quizzical elderly woman to whom he was introduced as her son. And then the 50-year-old John hugged and held his 84-year-old mother for the first time and they cried together. She would die three months later but, at last, he really had succeeded in finding his family.

If you can quit
for a day, you
can quit for a
lifetime.

BENJAMIN ALIRE SÁENZ

ONE DAY AT A TIME

Jan Cantle

My husband is a compulsive gambler. He was addicted to fruit machines, but now, thanks be, he has not gambled for more than 40 years.

I wrote this just before he got his one-year pin from Gamblers Anonymous in 1989. Searching for some family photographs, I came across the handwritten document.

> It was a shock when he admitted to me just how badly he was addicted. I had always known he liked to play the machines, but not that he was feeding them £30 to £50 a week. He had a good job, and I was working but there never seemed to be an end to the bills or the overdraft.
>
> One day, the bailiffs called about a gas bill that I thought had been paid by monthly direct debit. I asked him about it, and the whole story came out. He was in tears, I was stunned. Help was sought, first from the GP, and then from Gamblers Anonymous (GA). My husband had fallen ill in the last few weeks with ME and the doctor's reaction was to blame the symptoms on the gambling.

We sat and went through the bills. There were many that I had thought had been paid. Instead, they had ended as County Court Judgements against me, as they were in my name from the days when I was working and he was a student. I felt hurt, shocked, betrayed. We needed to clear the worst of them, £5000 in total. I dragged him to the CAB for debt counselling.

He asked me not to let him have a penny more in his pocket than he needed each day. We arranged that both signatures would be needed at the bank. All the time, I tried to be supportive — I had married for 'better or worse'.

He went to GA each week and found it helpful, but all along I was screaming inside. All the help seemed to be directed to the addict — no one seemed to understand the partner's needs. And I was ashamed — I had no need to be — and I did not understand why. I was not the one with the illness.

Our relationship had been deteriorating before he dropped this bombshell; I had suspected he had a relationship with another lady, never dreaming it was with Lady Luck.

We looked at the debts and decided to pay them off at a rate equivalent to his gambling — after all, we had not had the use of that money when it was feeding the machines. After a few months we had paid off a few debts of under £100 each. I started giving him cash to spare again. To live today he had to learn to have money in his hand. This he managed by actively avoiding places with fruit machines; if he saw them he started shaking with desire. If anybody ever tries to tell me gambling addiction and withdrawal causes no physical symptoms I won't believe them. Even a handful of coins had the same effect.

Having given up the habit, one day at a time, his personality changed. He was again the kind, considerate, loving man I had married. Even the children noticed the difference, and asked what had come over him. It was difficult to know what to tell them. At twelve and eight they were too young to understand, but their help was needed when we went on our first family holiday. I said that I wanted them to distract his attention when he went towards the machines. They did this brilliantly, and went for walks and snacks they didn't really want.

I found I could not cope alone, and in tears at 3 a.m. I wrote to the children's godmother. She was enormously supportive to both of us, writing to us and praying for us. I could not have managed without those letters — she wrote two or three times a week at first and this helped me to keep my sanity.

Next week GA will recognize the fact that he has not gambled for over a year. I am aware how hard that has been and I am proud that, one day at a time, has got us this far. We've got the debts under control and have just finished paying off one of the big ones. We've got another two years paying to go — but we will manage.

Now, I am getting depressed. I couldn't last year; my strength was needed to support him and the family through a crisis but, oh, the price! I've had to give up work because of failing health and feel hurt that this condition was exacerbated by last year's worry. But we are winning. It is possible to overcome addiction to gambling. The family of the gambler should not be ashamed. Feel proud, instead, every day that Lady Luck is ignored by the compulsive gambler.

I went to a couple of open meetings with him. There were very few family members there to see people get their hard-won awards. You might imagine the room as full of losers and down-and-outs. Instead, it was a room of incredible, brave people. They had acknowledged their problem. One day at a time, they were taking back control of their lives.

The phrase 'one day at a time' is most famous from the twelve-step program initially introduced for alcoholics, and then added to other groups battling addiction. It has become a mantra to use whenever difficulties arrive in life — to be honest, it is the only way I can cope with my husband's dementia.

It is now 2018. And he has not gambled since I first wrote this in 1988. I would like to dedicate it to all those people and families who have been touched by the evil of gambling addiction — keep on, there is life after gambling.

Sadly he has dementia now, and will not be seeing this — he would not comprehend it. But I feel it is important to share the story, a true story of struggle and success. I have asked for his permission to share the story, and he consented as well as he could.

You are **never too old** to set another goal or to dream a new dream.

C.S. LEWIS

IT'S NEVER TOO LATE

Renate Krakauer

My mother was 59 years old when she went back to school. Before the Holocaust had destroyed her family and her hopes for the future, she had studied pharmacy in Prague. After the war, she made her way to Canada with my father and me, a seven year old, to start a new life in a country where they didn't know anyone and couldn't speak the language.

We landed in Montreal on a cold blustery December night, taken in by kind strangers who had volunteered to help us over the first hurdles of getting settled. After finding a three-room walk-up flat and enrolling me in school, my parents registered in English classes in the evenings in a nearby high school. My father soon found work, his engineering degree from Prague and his European work experience helping him to get a professional start. My mother, however, was not so lucky. For licensing as a pharmacist in Quebec, my mother would have to take exams in French and work for a specified period of time in a pharmacy. That very word scared her. In Europe, a pharmacy was a professional store, dispensing prescriptions and a limited amount of over-the-counter remedies. In Montreal, it looked more like a mini department store to my mother. The manager soon put her to work — sweeping the floor and dusting the shelves. This first obstacle was psychological, a real blow to her self-esteem. She had never had to do that before.

The second obstacle was more difficult. My mother had to learn French. Having just started English classes, this was too much for her. Sadly, she put her dream on hold, spending her time looking after me and my father.

Fast forward twenty years. My parents were now living in Hamilton, Ontario. I was married with three children in nearby Toronto. My mother spent her time reading, knitting, watching soap operas and daydreaming. She was not one to join women's clubs. She lacked the self-confidence to volunteer, since most of the volunteers she met seemed to be fundraisers for one cause or another. One day when she was shopping in a local department store, she happened to pass by the pharmacy. There was the pharmacist in a white jacket dispensing a prescription. She was mesmerized. My father, who had gone into another part of the store, came back to get her and broke through her trance. When he asked her what the matter was, she said, 'That's where I want to be. I want to work behind the counter again.'

That's how her odyssey began. First she found out from the nearest Faculty of Pharmacy what she would have to do in order to resume her professional role. She was informed that she had to write a letter to the dean and get a letter of support from a practising pharmacist. Overcoming her natural shyness, she did both. When she was called in for an interview with the dean and his committee, they asked why she wanted to become a licensed pharmacist after all those years. She explained how she had loved her profession and how much she missed helping patients.

Finally the dean said, 'You know that at your age most people are contemplating retirement?'

Without hesitation, she replied, 'I'm not ready to die yet.'

My mother was accepted as a student in the Faculty of Pharmacy at the University of Toronto in 1970. She had to make up three third-year courses and two fourth-year courses. I remember her telling me that one of the science-based courses had not even been on the syllabus in her day. Not being a driver, she commuted by bus for the one-hour trip from Hamilton to Toronto two or three times a week as required. Having a hearing impairment, she was concerned that she might miss some of the professors' lectures. She needn't have worried. Her young classmates were so fond of her that they saved a seat for her in the front row for the lectures they knew she would be attending.

After finishing her coursework, including writing all the exams, my mother sat for the licensing exams. She passed and was admitted to practise in 1973 when she was 62 years old. She worked for ten years until she and my father decided to take a well-earned retirement. Those ten years were a highlight of her life.

When I wrote an obituary upon the death of my mother for the *Globe and Mail*, a national newspaper in Canada, I mentioned this wonderful accomplishment. A couple of years later, I received an email from the editor who publishes these obituaries, forwarding to me correspondence from a woman in Victoria, British Columbia. This woman had read my account of my mother's return to school. It had made her cry. As a 50 year old, she had yearned to get her

Bachelor degree, but felt that she was too old. My mother's story inspired her and she wrote to tell me that she had just graduated.

❀

My own story occurred in 1999. My professional life had started back in 1963 as a pharmacist, following in my mother's footsteps. But I didn't share her passion for this important role in the healthcare team. Instead, after trying out community and hospital practice and even working in a pharmaceutical company as a quality control chemist, I changed direction completely. I enrolled in a Master of Environmental Studies program when my children were two, four and seven. Having a babysitter saved my sanity. I wasn't cut out to be a stay-at-home mom, even though I loved my children, and still do, more than anything in the world.

I then began a chequered career — in continuing education at a community college, in human resources for a municipal government and then for the provincial government, and finally as the president of a college providing specialized training for a variety of health technologists. Along the way, I became a single parent. Longing to go back to school (I really wanted to be a lawyer!), I didn't because I couldn't afford to stop working. Although I received some child support from the children's father, I was the primary support for my children. Before I knew it, however, the years flew by and the children grew up. I no longer felt the constraint to support them financially. In addition, the Chair of the Board of the college I worked for suggested that when I retired, they would have to hire someone with a doctorate.

Before I knew it, I said, 'I'd have a doctorate if I had the time to write my thesis.'

'What do you mean?' he asked.

'I have been taking one course a year towards the requirements for my doctorate in adult education, but I would need to spend one year in full-time study to write my thesis.'

'You've got it!' he said, setting my heart to pounding with fear. What had I just committed to? Was I crazy? Who writes a thesis in twelve months?

My board chair, a dear man, took a proposal to the board to grant me a sabbatical so that I could proceed towards my doctorate. With their approval, I frantically started the process of registration at the Ontario Institute for Studies in Education at the University of Toronto. I had to write a letter persuading the dean to accept my application after finding a senior educator who would write to support me. I was 58 years old and I was following in my mother's footsteps!

I found a wonderful faculty advisor who steered and advised me throughout as I wrote my thesis — seven chapters, a lengthy bibliography and 327 pages in all — and the design of an assessment vehicle which I tested out and subsequently had published to modest acclaim in the Canadian college community. I passed my oral exam without needing to make a single correction and graduated at the age of 60. I must admit that sometimes I still feel like an imposter calling myself Dr Krakauer!

I have been a believer in lifelong learning all of my adult life. My mother was a great role model. I'm still learning, having published my first novel in 2015 at the age of 74 and currently working on my second. I truly believe that it's never too late!

The cave you
fear to enter
holds the **treasure**
you seek.

JOSEPH CAMPBELL

SNOW WHITE

Susie Anderson

On my desk upstairs is a scrap of paper with a stick figure drawing of a box and underneath are the words, 'HOW TO TURN ON'.

In the beginning I didn't want to be left alone with it. Actually, to be truthful, I didn't want to look at it at all. It took incredulous cries from my friends. 'What? You haven't got a computer!'

Then one day I was brutally shoved into my son's car and driven to a store — a place with masses of bewildering technology winking and blinking.

I was a great embarrassment to this son. Not only did I not have a computer but I also use the microwave for storing cookbooks and I had a landline and a smartphone with sticky tape holding it together.

I had tried.

I hopped on a tram and went to a store in the city once, stood there with flushed cheeks while young salespeople, who should have been playing outside in the fresh air, spoke to me about megabytes and ROMs and hardware. The only hardware I knew was a lovely place in South Melbourne where charming older men in grey coats called Bob or Fred climbed a ladder and reached onto the top shelf and found me a nail or a doorknob or picture hooks.

And what were the discs this young salesperson in the hi-tech shop was talking about? Did he mean the ones I listened to on my CD player as, apron on, music blaring, I cooked up a storm in the kitchen, waltzing around between the pots and pans?

I had tried.

I listened to my computer-savvy friends who lured me inside their homes on the pretext of lunch but then sat me down in front of a box that hummed in an evil way. They gazed adoringly at this box like they were in love, caressing a round thing they called a mouse and in breathy voices whispered, 'See? Look what you can do!'

Then they proceeded to show me endless photos of their grandchildren, little Johnny or Elly on the swings or making sand castles.

I sneaked out the door, un-noticed, as they, with fingers flying over the keys, went on the internet saying, 'It's just so fascinating'.

Well, I thought, driving home, *my fascinating moments will be swimming in a lagoon on the island of Malolo Lailai in Fiji or climbing a red escarpment under a blazing blue sky in the Kimberleys, not hunched and drooling over a computer.*

But there I was with my son in that whizzbang shop, with him propelling me firmly forward. He slithered over to a salesperson who looked about twelve and I distinctly heard my son say, 'Now look, make sure you deal with me, not my mother. She isn't into all this.'

I must admit the young sales person looked alarmed. The son then spoke to me very slowly with a rising inflection, like you do to a young child or someone who is very ill.

'Now Mum, trust me. One day this computer will be your friend.'

Can you believe I bought it? I was too afraid I wouldn't get home if I didn't!

I went mad. I also bought a printer and I did get a bit nostalgic when the salesperson spoke of ink cartridges. I had a flashback to school and the old inkwells and how we used to flick bits of paper dipped in the ink at each other. The talk of laser printing confused me. I had a friend who had laser surgery. I wish you could have seen the salesperson's face when I told him about my friend who after the surgery had one side of her face lower than the other.

For a week or so, those massive boxes of technology sat at the bottom of my stairs until the son, visiting one day, suggested he carry the boxes up the stairs to my desk and unpack them. Did I have a choice?

We sat there side by side, me smiling, nodding, as he instructed me in how it all worked. Me pretending I was full of enthusiasm to begin this new adventure.

I managed to avoid eye contact as I passed by the desk for about a week until one rainy gloomy day with nothing planned I sat down in front of the grey box, stared at the screen and bravely turned it on. It made a gentle singing sound and said, 'Hello'. And when I made an error it said, 'Okay, now let's go back to where you know'.

I called it Snow White because she was pretty scared at first but in the end it turned out just fine. I have invited some friends over later. I want to show them what Snow White and I can do together.

Ninety per cent of life is about remaining calm.

DR CHRIS FEUDTNER

MERREDIN

Barbara Mitchinson

In 1957 my husband accepted a position as an oil company representative in Merredin, a wheatbelt town in Western Australia, 163 miles from the capital city of Perth. We were in our twenties with a ten-month-old baby.

Our weekly income was £19. We had no savings but bought a new Holden car and our first house on a total deposit of £50. The bank manager shook his head, proclaiming we'd never make it.

In those days, 163 miles was considered quite a distance so my husband travelled ahead to look for suitable accommodation, keeping me up to date via letters. I should have kept those letters because today they would be classified as grounds for litigation!

He wrote that there were only two houses for sale: one for £3500 (quite out of the question) and the other £1300. The latter, he assured me, would be great and had an enclosed veranda along one side, ideal for a crawling baby. I trusted him, packed up our meagre possessions and travelled with the removalists to my new home, full of expectations. Those expectations soon disappeared, to be replaced with apprehension.

From the outside the house seemed reasonable enough if not slightly daunting, with a high front fence and a veranda enclosed with bright green corrugated iron. The front door was conspicuous too, the welcoming knocker being a massive lion's head made of iron. Visitors didn't enter quietly! Our new home had originally been a Kalgoorlie miner's cottage, one of many relocated throughout the wheatbelt when the gold rush abated. Built of asbestos, the interior walls were patterned stamp metal, over which some misguided person had pasted fawn wallpaper, now discoloured with age. For a toddler it was a magic game: poke your finger in and all these little holes appeared. It was exciting.

The kitchen (I knew it was a kitchen because there was an old black and silver wood stove on the far wall) had no water or sink, but it did boast a bench with a linoleum top and curtains hung on a wire in lieu of cupboard doors.

And the bathroom! The bathroom was to die for. I started to laugh (hysterically); my husband appeared genuinely puzzled and hurt. But hear me out! The bath was covered in clusters of rust (we learnt to squat). There was an old chip heater which regularly overflowed and spat boiling water. It simply could not cope with the mallee root wood chips used for heating. The pièce de résistance, however, would have to be the 'vanity basin'. An old grey sideboard adorned with several small drawers, each with a brass handle. Someone had inserted an enamel basin into the counter top. This in turn had an outlet big enough for your index finger (no plug). Washing your face became an act of dexterity.

Did I mention a side veranda? It opened from the kitchen and at first glance appeared to be the one saving grace. Curiously, the front wall was stacked to sill height and about a metre wide with old newspapers. Naturally I got rid of them, only to discover later that the façade was basically masonite which crumbled in the first winter downpour. Hence the stack of newspapers.

That first winter was interesting on several counts. It didn't take long to discover that there was a total of seven holes in the roof, through which the rain steadily dripped. No matter, problems are there to be solved and we soon had a good system in place. Two buckets and five containers were all it took to quell the downpour. I remember the first one to be rushed into place was over the marital bed. Made for some interesting nights, I can tell you!

The major challenge, however, was the toilet — or rather, dunny. For dunny it was: a long way from the house and backing onto a lane. The 'dunny man' changed the receptacle every week and no matter how hard he tried, you could smell that 'dunny man' wherever he went — even on the golf course.

I digress. I remember the ignominy of standing up and hearing the back flap drop into place and a group of local children laughing as they ran up the lane. A new bum in town! I was mortified. 'Give me a real toilet or …' I threatened.

It took six weekends of labouring over a soak well, chipping away at ground that was virtually rock, before I had a proper toilet, complete with a chain — and an exhausted husband.

A tap in the kitchen became rather a sore point. I had been told gently but firmly, that as the ground was so hard and sloping upwards it would be impossible for the water to drain away. I swallowed this story for about three years, carting water into the kitchen from an outside tap and then emptying it outside again. Then on one very wet afternoon while I was having an afternoon nap (as you do when seven months pregnant) my dearly beloved drove downtown, came back with the necessary and when I awoke, triumphantly showed me his handiwork. We had running water in the kitchen. To say that I was mad as hell probably doesn't even come close!

Over time the bath was replaced, the seven leaks in the roof patched up and with a tap installed in the kitchen and a real toilet, we had ourselves a palace. We were so proud we even painted it a pale mauve! Can you believe that?

I remember clearly entertaining our farming friends one evening and showing off our new gadget — an electric frypan. They were amazed to watch me make toasted sandwiches in it. At that stage electricity was not available in regional areas; farms were operated with generators.

The fun we had in those years! We travelled to dances in remote tiny towns, bedding our kids down in the back of station wagons; tennis was played on Sundays and then there were the 'tin-kettlings.' Tin-kettlings were an old tradition to welcome newlyweds on farms whereby their 'friends' would arrive (uninvited) in a convoy, tins and pans tied to car bumpers. Newlyweds knew it would happen, they just didn't know when.

No story of this era would be complete without mentioning the football — Aussie rules, of course.

Everyone gathered for the weekly game of football. Kids played together; young mums provided sumptuous afternoon teas; the players changed and showered in a tin shed (water heated by a mallee root fire, same result as at home). Win or lose, the footy was the highlight of the week. After the game the players gathered at the local pub to dissect the game kick by kick. Back then it was unheard of for women to enter pubs so we wives were left outside to feed fractious and tired babies. Life in the 1950s!

The five years we spent in Merredin were golden. We learnt to stand on our own two feet, to make our own decisions and to budget on an impossibly small wage. We learnt the real values in life, and the best gift of all? We made lifelong friendships, which are as real today as they were back then.

I am not afraid of the storms for I am learning how to sail my ship.

LOUISA MAY ALCOTT

WEIGHT TILL YOU SEE ME NOW

Teresa Fenton

Megan is now 30 but when she looks back over her young years, she blushes and shudders. She had always been a chubby little girl. The only child of her adoring parents, Bob and Bernie, and the first grandchild to arrive to swell and gladden the hearts of granny and grandad on both her mum's and dad's sides of the family. Both parents were slightly overweight, so the issue of weight was never a topic of conversation in their lovely, happy house. Megan did notice, though, that at school she could never run as fast as her classmates. She somehow felt that to try to talk about this at home would not be a good idea. Megan loved the ways her mum always comforted her when she was sad — she got lots of warm hugs as her mother enfolded her between her huge soft breasts and her plump arms and kissed her fondly. She also gave her a bag of sweets or a bar of her favourite chocolate.

One type of sweets she really loved actually looked like miniature cushions! Her emotions were being cushioned and comforted by them and also by the countless times she was cocooned and held to her mum's soft, kind, plump chest, full of love. Another favourite was a 'soother', a boiled sweet made entirely of hard sugar. Oh, she could suck for hours on that heavenly treat. Megan was quite happy that she had a soft, comfortable body, like her mum had — for as long as she was in her small country primary school, that is.

Almost as soon as she began to attend the huge secondary school in the town a mile away, Megan's external world got bigger but she got smaller inside. The crumbling feeling crept in, in small ways at first. She saw two girls pointing at her tummy and giggling together. Megan did not understand why, but she did know they were laughing at her. She often hid in the toilet and cried a lot. Each day she tried in vain to make friends, smiling and waving at the other girls, but all of the slim, agile girls seemed to only have interest in each other. She felt alone and unwanted and often looked at herself in the mirror at home to see if she could see what was so ugly about her. She even considered asking them what she could do to stop them from laughing at her and make them want to be her friend. She did not find the courage.

Shame began to ooze from her skin. It wrote its name in red raw pimples on her face. The intense daily agony was a heavy weight on her young vulnerable shoulders, which began to fold inwards. The pain of the ridicule was acute, but equally sharp was the pain of the next anticipated onslaught. Again, she decided it was best not to ask her mum why they might be laughing at an innocent twelve-year-old girl. She was soon to find out with the acuity and clarity of a scalpel to the heart.

When Megan was thirteen, Facebook and Twitter became all the fashion. While her parents wanted to retain Megan's innocence for a while longer, her tears and red swollen eyes melted their hearts and they reluctantly allowed her to join, on her new iPhone. Megan's face brightened and she was thrilled with her new social tool that might help her to make friends.

While she daily suffered the secret, sharp, silent pain of her unknown misdemeanour, she could not have imagined what was to come. The silent torture was replaced by very vocal punishment and she was now very clear as to why. One of the 'smart' girls had taken a photo of Megan and had put it up on Facebook. The comments that they included made Megan's stomach sick and her whole body go weak and powerless when she read them. A few times she vomited at school with sheer emotional torment when she thought of some of the names she was called: 'fat pimply pig', 'pregnant rhino' and 'greedy culchie cow'.

On the fifth day of April, a month before her thirteenth birthday, Megan decided to starve herself. If it meant she would die, so what? She had died inside already.

With each successful starvation day, she astonished herself that she was becoming more and more devious. She could pretend to eat her lovely tasty dinner, saying 'yummy' to her mum while putting most of it into her pockets, to dump when her unsuspecting parents were not looking. She bought bathroom scales and hid them in the bottom of her bedside cupboard. Food was now her enemy and the scales, her best friend, brought her good news every day. If she got tempted to eat some food, she always reminded herself of the sinking shame and suffering that her schooldays had become. As she noticed how fast the kilos were dropping from her body, she often felt elated at this huge secret success that was hers and hers alone. A few times she avoided dinner at home by telling her parents that she had had dinner at her 'friend's' house. It also happened a few times that the amazing smell of her mother's tasty cooking became too much for her. She ate her entire dinner, but felt so full of guilt, failure and self-hate that she had to take action. Vomiting was now an option. It was no stranger to her. She sneaked off to the bathroom and pushed her index and middle fingers down her throat until she managed to vomit it up. This 'triumph' restored her feelings of control and optimism.

As Megan's ribs were now bare of flesh and very obvious, she began to fear that her parents would notice and comment on the many long walks and jogs that were becoming her habit lately. This could lead them to suspect her eating disorder. An urgent change of plan was required. Now that she had perfected the art of purging, she could eat most of her dinner and then put plans A and B into action — go out for a vigorous run and, at a secluded spot, vomit up her dinner.

One evening, as Megan came through the hallway at home after this abusive routine had been completed, she felt her head become like a TV with no reception and her legs begin to tremble and collapse like a house of cards. She did not know why she had hit the floor, or why she was waking in a hospital bed.

As part of her treatment she was weighed, and the nurse gasped when she discovered that Megan only weighed 6 stone 2 pounds. Her parents were summoned and felt distraught when she told them the whole tragic story of how she was trying to starve herself to death, because it was her escape from her torture and turmoil.

She was moved to the eating disorders ward and put under gentle professional care. There she slowly learnt how to eat healthy amounts of nourishing foods, cut out the foods that she once considered to be comforting, and achieve a normal body weight for her age and height. Now she had a new sense of healthy control in her life. The entire trauma got Bernie thinking about her own weight and how she was not a great example to Megan. She started 'stay slim' classes in her local community centre. At difficult times, she reminded herself of Megan's frightening situation and lost 3 stone, now feeling like a new woman.

When Megan eventually returned to school, she was a confident and different Megan, both outside and inside. Meantime, a lot had happened at school, too. Her parents had visited and informed the principal of the tragedy that was averted, revealed the social media comments that their daughter had been subjected to, and insisted that action be taken. It was. The girls responsible were suspended and ordered to attend counselling sessions to heal the emotions that were at the root of their cruel behaviour.

Second year, and all of her following years, became Megan Heaven. Her open, soft personality made her three genuine close friends, whom she saw as her soulmates. Her study routine became a pleasure that she rewarded with a lovely bike ride in the cool fresh air each day by the river. She felt so grateful that there was no stop to puke behind a tree as in the past. Every day of her new life she felt an overwhelming sense of thankfulness for the love of her parents, the hospital care, her new friends, and her two major successes — high marks in her exams and her new healthy body.

Three months before her eagerly anticipated leaving certificate examination, over a healthy dinner of meat and lots of mixed vegetables, Megan's parents asked her what profession might be her first choice as her life career. Without hesitation, Megan replied, 'I want to be an eating disorder therapist so I can help girls like me.'

The world only exists
in your eyes. You can
make it as big or
as small as you want.

F. SCOTT FITZGERALD

HOW DID A GIRL LIKE ME END UP IN A PLACE LIKE THIS?

Dr Meryl Broughton

For a while I felt like a fraud, sitting there behind the desk telling people to eat their broccoli and go for a walk every day. Many years later I discovered my experience had a name, 'Imposter Syndrome'.

Doubt about my abilities and the qualifications that entitled me to instruct a person on what they should or should not do sprung out of two separate moments of career crisis.

The saga started with pickled brains. Not mine; some brains whose owners had finished using them. These organs removed at autopsy were carefully suspended in buckets of preservative. Others already processed in formalin were sliced and laid out on trays ready for inspection by a neuropathologist, the laboratory medical specialist of brains and nerve tissue. I saw these strange sights on a tour of Pathology House, a former domestic dwelling that had been converted into a small research centre for conditions of the nervous system.

This exposure to pathology, the intersection between health and disease, could have inspired me to become a doctor. But it didn't. I only went into medicine because I was smart enough and a diligent student. And the careers guidance officer at my high school told me to apply.

The first three pre-clinical years were full of fun things: frog's legs in Ringer's lactate, anaesthetized rabbits, organic chemistry, dunking other students into water to measure lean body mass, dissecting formaldehyded body donors, gazing at organs in acrylic boxes, inspecting articulated skeletons and many other odd pursuits.

Though the learning was strenuous, it was stimulating and exciting. Each year when I passed the exams, I looked forward to the next year. It was a bit competitive, because if you failed you were out. There were no second chances to continue in that specific degree course.

But the last three clinical years were something else. In this stage we were introduced to the key element of medical practice: the patient.

Seeing patients when I was a medical student caused me no end of anxiety. A large part of my difficulty was asking permission of the head nurse in charge of the ward to see 'Mr Jones' or any other patient with those fantastic clinical signs that every student should examine. Inevitably, it seemed I was the straw that broke the camel's back, whether that was the irritated nurse or the exhausted patient.

If I wasn't flatly refused, I became wracked by guilt for causing so much grief to the hospital staff and patients. I began to wonder how I could possibly have come so far through such a long university course when I was clearly unsuited to the job. I didn't like people. Even worse, I didn't like sick people.

Not only that, our informal small-group tutor, a medical registrar, thought I was too nervous during my practice case presentations. 'You should take beta blockers,' was his declared solution.

Great. Instead of giving encouragement and guided support, he implied I was so hopeless the only way to fix me was with pharmaceuticals. I felt pathologically flawed. I became distressed and despondent, wondering how it had got so bad, how I could feel so 'stuck'. I went to see someone with experience in counselling the distressed and despondent.

The wise counsel I received helped me to see that I wasn't stuck. I could move on to something else, somewhere else. The study I had done so far would never be wasted, just used differently. Knowing I could actually quit medicine at any time and go do something else relieved me of performance pressure, without the need for medication.

Despite all that angst in my undergraduate medical training, I passed my final exams ranked in the middle of my cohort. But it wasn't plain sailing from there. The work was intensive and arduous. The hours were long and gruelling. There were still hospital wards and head nurses and sick patients.

The time came to pursue specialist training. I chose anatomical pathology. Perhaps those bucketed brains had a more lasting impact on me than I consciously recalled. This medical field involves patients in a more indirect way. Diagnoses are made by examining parts removed at surgery and tissues under the microscope. When interacting with whole humans, it was to do surgery when no anaesthetic is required, at post mortem.

Performing autopsies became my delight. Exploring the marvels of the body and solving the mysteries that caused individual deaths made sense to me and felt right. But despite my preference for the laboratory, I was destined to become a 'real' doctor.

The rigours of training for pathology had also got the better of me. It wasn't lack of capability but logistics that tripped me up again. After-work lectures were held in the city centre. I was working out in the suburban 'sticks' of a peripheral hospital. Tutorials and study groups flitted around the big inner-city hospitals and I was often not informed of location changes. This was the era before the world was at our fingertips with mobile communication devices. Too much of my precious time and energy became consumed in travel.

Back in those days it was possible to go into general medical family practice without any particular specialist training for it. So that is what I did.

My sensitivities to the feelings of others, which caused me so much struggle at the start, enabled my success as a family doctor. Now I don't have to beg anyone to see patients: they *pay* to see me. I've made a career out of listening to their concerns and helping them deal with their health problems. It would appear that I got over my hang-ups with humans.

In a rather interesting turn of events, the opportunity to return to my first medical love appeared when I was working in a rural area. Due to my unusual training and experience in anatomical pathology, and my enthusiasm for the post-mortem examination, I was able to embellish my role as a country doctor by performing autopsies for the local coroner.

This ancillary field of medical practice for me did not last indefinitely. Times changed and it became no longer suitable for generalists to perform such a specialist service. And the old regional hospital was replaced with a new one that did not have an autopsy room! However, it was satisfying to utilize those skills for several years that at another stage I thought might be wasted.

As I have come to realize and can therefore, in turn, counsel others: no study, training or experiences are ever really wasted. They may just be used differently from what you might have thought. Even now I can still move on to something else, somewhere else. Perhaps I can entertain and educate people with tales of medical adventures that explain why they should eat their broccoli and go for a walk every day?

All **progress** takes place outside the comfort zone.

MICHAEL JOHN BOBAK

HONOUR THY FATHER AND MOTHER

Joyce C. Assen

The year was 1944 and the war in Europe was drawing to a close but life in small-town Ontario was still hard, especially for one little girl named Betty. Her parents had met a few years before at a religious conference. They were devoted to each other and their church and raised their children to abide by the tenets of their chosen religion.

Betty loved her parents and like most six year olds she desperately wanted to please them, so she tried hard to accept the teachings of her parents' religion. But sometimes it was very difficult.

Unlike other fathers who'd volunteered to serve their country, Betty's dad hadn't. His faith forbade it. He accepted the stares of the other townsfolk, who behind his back called him a coward for not doing his duty. Unfortunately for Betty, these comments were repeated so often in her classmates' homes that children taunted her about this too, which hurt her deeply as she knew her father was a good man.

The other tenet of her parents' faith that Betty found difficult to accept was their non-observance of Christmas. To them, Christmas was nothing more than pagan rituals so there were no

Christmas trees, no music, no presents and no feasting. Christmas was simply a day like any other.

Unfortunately for Betty, the world around her did celebrate in a big way, complete with a Christmas concert at school. At her parents' request she was allowed to leave school while the other kids stayed behind to practise Christmas carols in preparation for the concert, which, of course, she wasn't allowed to attend.

It was one of those days in early December when she was sent home early when Betty came up with her idea. Maybe she couldn't take part in the concert, nor expect any presents, but what she could do was have her own Christmas tree. After all, her parents' home was located at the edge of town right next to a large wooded area, which held lots of fir trees of varying sizes. All she needed were decorations. She thought and thought about this and finally came up with another idea. Her mother had a large sewing basket filled with buttons, ribbons and lace, and Betty surmised her mother would never notice if a few went missing. She was all set — now all she had to do was wait for an appropriate time.

On the Saturday before Christmas the opportunity presented itself. It required that she make up a story, so she told her mom she was going to a friend's house to play. Her mother was pleased as Betty was seldom invited to her classmates' homes.

The day was crisp and cold with a light snow falling when Betty headed into the woods, her pockets filled with bits of ribbon, lace, thread and buttons. She wore the brown woollen coat her mother had cut down for her. It was something her mother had picked up at the annual church bazaar. The coat was warm and came down to the top of her boots. But she hated it and even though her mother had tried to modernize it with rows of trim at the collar, on the cuffs and at the bottom, it still looked like a hand-me-down. On her head she had a small knitted hat her mother had made for her. It was bright red with knitted pompoms on the ties, making it easier for a little girl to tie.

Betty left the house around 1 p.m. It took only about fifteen minutes to find the perfect tree. It was small, only about 4 feet tall, a little taller than the wee girl who was going to decorate it. It was a hard task to accomplish with tiny hands bundled in red woollen mittens, which, of course her mother had knitted. In about a half an hour her work was completed and Betty stood back to admire the finished product. It looked so pretty; not as grand as the one decorated in the window of the general store but still beautiful, especially with freshly fallen snow glistening on its branches.

Betty then sang a carol she had heard the other children practising at school. 'Oh Christmas tree, oh Christmas tree, how lovely are thy branches.' As she sang she realized that tears were streaming down her cheeks and freezing to her face. She wasn't sure why she was crying but more than likely it was the unfairness of it all. She wanted desperately to fit in and do all the things the other kids did at Christmas time. She wanted the decorated tree, she wanted the carols, she wanted her home filled with the scent of Christmas baking, and she even wanted presents. Most of all she pined for the dolly in the window of the general store; the one who could walk and say 'Mama'. She felt very conflicted because on one hand, she desperately yearned to please her parents, but on the other, she wanted all the things that her peers took for granted at this special time of year.

Later that day, just as sun was setting, she headed home. Quizzed by her mother as to how things went at her friend's house, she said she'd had fun. It was one of the few times in her young life she remembered lying and although she suffered some pangs of guilt, she concluded it was for a good cause.

Several times during the Christmas holidays, Betty made the trek into the woods to see her tree. Just before heading back to school in the new year, she took down the ribbons, lace and buttons and buried them in a snowbank. She thought of her tree often in childhood and then as a teenager she buried it deep in her subconscious.

Later in life, when Betty married and had children of her own, Christmas took on a new significance. She would often describe it as 'making up for lost time'. Decorations went up early and stayed up until well after the new year. Her home was filled with the smell of candles and Christmas baking. Carols blared from the stereo all day. In short, it was a complete assault on all the senses.

The Christmas tree reached right to the ceiling and was beautifully decorated. The floor beneath its branches was filled with presents. There were presents for everyone they knew, and as they had a great many friends there were always lots of gifts. It wasn't that they were wealthy, it was just that Christmas was a priority they saved up for all year.

Every year on Christmas Eve, Betty insisted the whole family gather round the tree and sing, *Oh Christmas tree* and every year she cried. When their daughters were about five and six respectively, she sat them down after this annual ritual of homage to a tree and explained to them why it was so meaningful to her. Then she and her girls had a good cry together, followed by hugs and kisses all around.

Many Christmases came and went over the years. The girls got married and moved away. Eventually there were grandchildren to join in the festivities and, although the location of their Christmas celebration changed over the years, Betty and her husband continued to celebrate the season in grand style.

Looking back from an older person's perspective, Betty realized her little Christmas tree was only the first of many attempts to distance herself from her parents. The most crucial and final had come when she turned eighteen.

From the time she was six years old Betty had taken violin lessons, which her parents struggled to pay for. She couldn't even recall how the musical training began. Probably it was her parents' idea to provide some culture in their daughter's life. Even after they moved to another town miles away from where her music teacher lived, her dad continued to drive her back and forth, once a week, rain or snow. At eighteen, when she finished high school, Betty decided she had had enough. It was probably the most difficult conversation she ever had with her parents, informing them that she no longer wanted to study the violin. Her dad left the room and she and her mom just sat there and cried. This was to be her final expatriation, as she left home shortly after.

Later in life she would lose her mother and her father would remarry. She loved them both and as an adult she came to the realization that the decisions they'd made for her were made because they wanted the best for her. But ultimately only she could decide what would make her happy, and if that meant deviating from her parents' values, then so be it. In charting her own path and being independent, she truly 'honoured her father and mother'.

A truly **strong** person does not need the approval of others any more than a lion needs the approval of sheep.

VERNON HOWARD

WHAT'S THE DIFFERENCE?

Teresa Cannon

When we were children we were sent to the beach, not to play, not to swim, but to harvest a meal. We lived in a small coastal town — sleepy, with a few dusty streets and numerous wives who fretted that the high tides may claim their husbands as they embarked on their nightly fishing expeditions.

We were migrants. We did things differently. As children we were desperate to fit in and to hide our difference but we rarely succeeded. Language and customs do not change overnight. And worse, they emphasize, rather than diminish, difference.

Eating, how and what, was the most obvious custom that set us apart. We were regularly given buckets and directed to gather periwinkles and limpets. In 1960s Australia (and even today), marine snails were not actually considered gastronomical fare. So our gathering of periwinkles was ridiculed by the locals. We feared their stone throwing, their name calling, 'Pommie bastards'. We struggled with ourselves to hold our own but in spite of the common maxim that 'words will never hurt', they did. They seeped into our souls and found a permanent, bruising presence there. We knew we were less-than, and it hurt.

We were keen to keep our food-gathering excursions furtive affairs. We conceived elaborate strategies to mask our real purpose. We carried crab catchers to avert attention. Crabs were more acceptable fare than periwinkles. But buckets and rock scrambling quickly gave the game away and left us victim to more bullying.

We wasted no time on the harvest. Carefully, we plucked our prey. The spiral swirl of the periwinkles allowed for easy picking but the limpets resisted. Clinging to their spot, they clamped even more tightly once they detected a tug. I admired their resistance, wishing I could find similar stamina to deal with the jeering.

As soon as our buckets were full, we made a quick retreat home. There, we ran fresh water over the shells, removing sand and other debris, even the smell of the sea. Cooked and cooled, the little snails were carefully separated from their shells with a sewing needle. Piercing the bit that was just peeping from its shell, and holding the needle firmly, we twirled the shell until it released its meat. Tiny brown worms on bread — periwinkle sandwiches. The limpets suffered a similar fate, but being larger and rounder they sat clumsily on the bread. Periwinkles slid down the throat lubricated by butter on the bread, with sand remnants a crunchy addition. Limpets, like tough gristle, took some effort before they were chomped into swallowable bits.

How we hoped there'd be no visitors during periwinkle time. We always washed them quickly so we could secret them into the pot. If they were in the fridge and visitors called in, we feared their horror should they see them. We feared the subsequent ridicule.

As hard as we tried to hide our differences, different we were, and everyone knew. Difference was worse than sin. We were, after all, not real Australians. Our parents came from overseas. 'Back home' they called it, which was very confusing for us. We thought this was home, here, where we lived. Catholic we were, but not real Catholics. We weren't Irish. We were Pommies.

But visitors did come and invariably they caught us — eating periwinkles. How shameful! How scandalous! We knew that gossip travelled through the town quicker than a virus. How would we, as eaters of periwinkles, ever face the townspeople again? Some visitors were kinder, gently coaxing us to more 'conventional' fare — oysters. Yes, if we were so enamoured with shellfish, surely we could shift our tastes to oysters.

'Just like eating snot,' my mother scorned.

There were the pigs' heads, the trotters, the lambs' tongues and the chicken soups of hearts, livers and legs. We ate them all. When visitors called in they were offered sandwiches of brawn or tongue. They recoiled in disgust while we children sat mortified and humiliated.

During the mullet season, we rose early and raced to meet the fishermen. With force and insistence, they propelled their boats across the last waves toward the sands. There, with abrupt and matter-of-fact manners, they slapped half a dozen of their catch into our buckets. Then they were off to the co-op to relinquish the remainder of their catch.

Back home, my mother snaffled the catch, scaled and gutted it with a dexterity that I envied.

We ate the fish for breakfast. No one else did that. But even worse, we ate the roe, the small sacks of eggs that my mother carefully removed from within the fish. For some reason she found it necessary to identify the gender of the fish according to its roe.

As she dropped each sack into the pan to cook, she'd announce 'male' if it was white and creamy; 'female' if it contained the little eggs. I saw no need for her genderizing. It only exacerbated our already weird position within the town. And it fuelled the struggle within.

'Mullet down the gullet,' we'd snigger to each other. This made light of what we were actually doing. At least the roe was consumed immediately, so such deviance and its consequent embarrassment were kept well concealed from our neighbours.

It's often said that difficult experiences can bring about meaning and understanding. And so it has been for me. In time I reflected on what had been. My mind opened. Bullying involves fear of the other, the fear of difference based, no doubt, on ignorance. Fear and ignorance can lead to the ridicule of others. Most importantly, there are the limitations that fear and ignorance impose. Restricted from entering into the new, the other, the different, one cannot embrace life with its many delights, its magic and its joys.

Years after leaving that small town, I eyed a fish as it stared back at me with its one eye. It was on a white plate swimming (metaphorically) in chilli sauce. I assumed it was chilli sauce since it was red and I was in the mountains of the southern Indian state of Kerala, where hot, spicy food is a popular cuisine.

A man was standing before me. He had delivered the fish with grace and pride. He had cooked it. Maybe he had even caught it from one of the many nearby streams. We spoke different languages but I wanted him to know how grateful I was. I looked at him with all the appreciation I could summon to my face. I knew he got my message.

I dug my fingers into the fish. My assumptions about the chilli were immediately confirmed. So practical the Indians, that they sense food first with fingers, then with the tongue. They have often expressed to me their amazement about western eating habits. Why limit our experience of food to sight and smell before putting it into our mouths? Why not savour with fingers the texture, dryness, moisture and smoothness? And why not check for the risk of bones before placing food into the mouth? For Indians, it is inconceivable that we forgo such experiences.

I sat in the tiny hut with its wooden benches and tables, all grey, no doubt from years of weathering. The coolness of the mud floor seeped into my feet and legs, giving relief from the heat. I hoped the breeze would not sprinkle dust or cobwebs onto my fish. I separated flesh from bones and placed the first morsel in my mouth. Even the heat of the chilli did not disguise the oily, fishy flavour. I ate slowly and determinedly. Tastewise, this was not the most enjoyable meal, but for generosity, hospitality and satisfaction of hunger, it was indeed perfect.

I still reflect on those childhood times of mullet roe, periwinkles, brawn and chicken legs, and the pain they caused. Each reflection brings deeper learnings. Such learnings have guided me through numerous meals, from sheep innards and mare's milk in Mongolia, fish heads in Singapore, to jellied eel in London. They have enabled me to enter into the difference of others and to enter such difference with joy and delight. I've received easy entree into many customs, rituals, languages, hospitality and, of course, food. I've been easy with the difference.

On the beach of my childhood I did indeed feel different, even alienated. But throughout my life, difference has served me well. Now I feast on it!

Strength and growth come only through continuous effort and struggle.

NAPOLEON HILL

FROM LOATHING TO LOVING ACADEMIA

Graham Lenton

History and war have been a fundamental part of my life. The following work is a condensed outline of the journey concluding with a degree in history and war studies.

Born in the early 1930s, my parents were witness to the bombing of Birmingham during World War II. From where they lived (Smethwick and Bearwood) the horizon glowed in November 1941 as Coventry burned. For varying reasons, both had unhappy childhoods. My mother left home at fifteen and lived in South Shields, County Durham. My father enjoyed National Service, enlisting with the 14/20th King's Royal Hussars. He later volunteered for bomb disposal and was based in Germany assisting in the removal of Allied ordnance. My parents resolved their children would never hear or see an argument between them and they kept that resolve until my father's passing.

My time in education was not an enjoyable experience; how things have changed. Those changes cover a host of issues and student welfare policies, which were very different to those of today. Two years at primary school began in 1963 and were not without trauma. Walking to school was not unusual, and on one such walk home a disagreement with three other classmates climaxed in a scuffle. Luck more than judgment saw me come out of it the better. Though not condoned, I was never bullied again during my school life. In another instant I was knocked unconscious after a fall in the playground. The headmistress put me on the couch in her study and told me to sleep it off! I need say no more on the health policy of the time.

In 1965 I walked to the local junior school. But it was the corporal punishment which left a lasting memory here. The majority of male teachers had served during the war and discipline was taken seriously. Punishment ranged from a flat-handed slap, the ruler, pump and cane. During dinner break, the headmaster's weapon of choice for those students who talked during his watch was a large soup ladle, which would land heavily on the cranium of the unsuspecting student. Behind the headmaster's house was an apple orchard, which was often raided (scrumping) by pupils as a 'dare'. Being caught resulted in 'three of the best', which I received only once. As Apollo 11 landed on the moon in 1969, I sat the eleven-plus exam. Being no great academic, I failed. I have no issue with this controversial exam; those of academic promise passed and I continued on to secondary school.

Now in a school uniform, that first day was daunting. Corporal punishment was still the deterrent, but here the deputy headmaster (known as Flash due to his once silver hair turned gold through smoking) would listen to the student before deciding if the cane should come out of the cupboard. Though strict, Flash was always fair. He was one of a handful of teachers who were genuinely liked by parents and students alike. My older sister attended the same school and was academically brighter than me, which affected my education during my second year. At the close of a geography lesson, the teacher asked in front of the class why I was not as clever as my sister. Overnight, all interest in education left me and my work reflected this. A brighter outlook occurred with the arrival of a new history teacher — his enthusiasm transferred onto the students. An interest in history has stayed with me ever since.

Away from education, there was social unrest. The miners' strikes of 1972 and 1974 caused major industrial disruption. Controlled electricity power cuts also affected family life; candle sales could not keep up with demand. The 1974 strike was a direct cause for the toppling of the Conservative government led by Prime Minister Edward Heath. Car manufacturer British Leyland was crippled by strike action throughout the 1970s. Union convenor Derek Robinson (known as Red Robbo) led the strike campaign. In 1977 Leyland was nationalized as a result of bankruptcy. Global events also had their impact: 1975, end of the Vietnam War; 1980, Iranian embassy; 1982, Falklands War; and 1989, the fall of the Berlin Wall.

At the age of twelve I was employed in part-time work, which would have sent the Health and Safety Executive into freefall. I worked in a vehicle breaker's yard. It was not unusual for me to be using an acetylene torch to cut engines out of old or damaged cars. Lessons on flammables and heavy objects were often learnt the hard way. Three evenings and Saturday mornings were taken up with this work until I left school. There can be no doubt my education suffered due to these activities, but at the age of sixteen my first new motorcycle was paid for in cash.

Leaving school in 1975, I was employed as an apprentice mechanic at a garage and remained there for fifteen years. The first year included a nine-week block release system at college. The feeling of being back in education was not what I expected. It took twelve months before the garage was notified I had not been attending, working instead at a motorcycle shop. I was given another chance by an understanding service manager. The following year, a day-release arrangement was introduced and I managed to attain 100 per cent attendance. The same service manager also advised staff to join a private pension plan, believing in years to come the state pension would be minimal. I was eighteen and now paying into a pension for a retirement which seemed a 'lifetime' away. At 23, while replacing an engine, an accident occurred that irreparably damaged my back. It was an injury that has to be managed carefully to this day.

Motorcycles continued to be a passion. I competed in production racing and for a short period worked as a motorcycle courier. It was cold, demanding work and with a young family the dangers of constant high-speed riding were always a concern. In 1990 we relocated to Cumbria, where I worked as a night warden on a holiday caravan site and my wife worked in the onsite shop. Due to the cost of housing, we had no choice but to return to the Midlands. Although in continual work, it was 1999 before I settled into long-term employment with one of the emergency services. Employed as a motorcycle mechanic, I gained promotions and rose to garage supervisor. Interest in history and war was never far away, and a motorcycle trip with work colleagues in 2001 took us to the World War I sites around Ypres and Mons. Trips to various locations continued over the following five years and fuelled the need to know more on the subject. In 2015, the availability of the private pension from so long ago made it possible to take early retirement. What to do next was a decision that needed the support of my wife and now grown children.

My wife and eldest daughter had already completed degrees and suggested I should follow the trend. An open day at Wolverhampton University confirmed I was qualified to enrol for a history and war studies degree. Our youngest daughter enrolled at the same time in games design. In September 2015 I walked through the doors of the university, and concerns of being a 'mature student' amongst so many young people were ill-founded. During the last three years I have met some truly wonderful people and through field courses visited many thought-provoking sites. The quality of lectures has been to a high standard. Wolverhampton is blessed with renowned experts in the studies of war. The lowest point of university life was the passing of my father in 2016. Again, my family were the ultimate support, but it was the kind reassurances from lecturers and fellow students that I was not prepared for. My youngest daughter and I graduated during the same week in 2018, and now understanding the depth of study required for a degree makes me all the more proud of a family who have stayed by my side through thick and thin.

In conclusion, as a youth I loathed education — if I was a 'slow burner' then it was an extremely long fuse. Be prepared to re-evaluate your initial preconceptions of your chosen studies; it will happen. Never think you are too old to learn and never be afraid of learning from those younger than yourself. If you have a question, ask it; with a room full of similar-minded students there will be someone thinking the same. Above all, enjoy the experience. Three years will pass quickly; the cap and gown will soon come. If at all possible, do not miss the graduation as it is an experience in itself and something to look back on with a sense of pride. I only wish my father had been there to see it.

The **bravest** thing I ever did was continuing my life when I wanted to die.

JULIETTE LEWIS

I'VE CHEERED UP SINCE THEN

Liana Joy Christensen

Is it possible to live your dreams across the lifespan? Even if your dreams appear to be stillborn before you have even become an adult? As a young person my expectations of life were lower than the proverbial snake's belly. My adolescence and early adulthood were full of angst. It's common enough, sadly. Our culture lacks effective rites of passage across the perilous straits from child to adult. Like so many young people I felt worthless, ugly and uncreative. In such a dark space, it was easy to be seduced by romantic notions of suicide. I flirted with razor blades, inscribing lines on my wrists that will be with me as long as I live.

I seldom think about them now. However, one day in my early professional career as an editor I was working side by side with a graphic designer, reviewing the images for an upcoming issue of our magazine. Out of the blue, she casually remarked, 'What are those? It looks like you tried to kill yourself.'

The question was clearly innocent and not intended to harm. My answer was equally blunt.

'I did.'

Her response was one that delighted me. Most people would have been nonplussed and deeply embarrassed by the unvarnished honesty of my answer, but she simply commented with wry insight. 'I guess you must have cheered up since then.'

I laughed. Indeed I had!

That conversation took place more than thirty years ago. And my cheerfulness remains undiminished. The life I wished to end at the age of nineteen has ended up being rich and strange. I am no longer surprised that it continues to startle and delight me with unlikely joys.

Take, for example, the fact I was recently offered my first professional gig — as a dancer. I began dance lessons as a two-and-a-half-year-old, but it was not something I had worldly ambitions about. Performing was for fun. Although I was strong and had excellent rhythm and balance, my body was never flexible, even as a preschooler, and now I'm 63! So how did I end up being paid for a weekend's work doing something at which I'm strictly amateur, amateur in the literal meaning *lover of*? Well, partly it was because of — not despite — my age.

Let me explain. A 60-year-old friend and myself were employed as part of a public relations stunt at a large convention and expo on aged care. The company that employed us were big on promoting being active and living your dreams throughout your life. It was a message I felt quite happy to support. Of course, to qualify for such a gig we had to actually be able to dance. In this regard, both our employers and we got more than we bargained for.

Their expectations of a rather staid duet were rapidly overturned as we took our places for the first time and segued from lyrical, to swing jazz to hip hop. The response was electric.

Passersby stopped and started filming us on their smartphones; some of them even filmed selfies with us dancing in the background. Staff from other stalls elsewhere in the exhibition heard about *the dancers* and came to see us perform in their break. The company we represented won the award for the best stall at the exhibition. The stall itself was set up as a relaxed coffee shop. It was beautiful and welcoming, but we supplied the X-factor. The judges commented, 'It was a no-brainer because of *the dancers*'.

Over the weekend, we performed our routine more than 30 times. Most members of the public were there to canvass care options for themselves or their loved ones, a necessary but not necessarily fun activity. And then the music started. And when we caught the eyes of a man or woman something more came in to the equation. Eyes lit up; feet were tapping; heads were nodding. So many people said, wistfully, 'Oh I used to dance' or, wonderingly, 'Maybe I could go back to dancing' or, amazedly, 'I didn't think it was possible for old people to do hip hop' (this last was my favourite!).

Our expectations were exceeded, too. It was delicious and unexpected to be, albeit briefly, 'professional dancers'. We were grateful to be given that guernsey. Grateful to our teachers and choreographers, one of whom played the role of our minder all weekend. And I am especially grateful for our two-member fan club: gap-toothed twins whose mother was working one of the stalls. The twins informed us that they did a dozen dance classes a week between them; and over the weekend they did not miss a single one of our performances. They were enchanted and enchanting. And whether or not they go on with their dance classes, and whether or not they remember us, I like to think they will be less likely to believe the lie that dancing, or life itself, is only for the young and thin. Their expectations won't be arbitrarily limited.

There is no use-by date on fun, creativity and relevance. Nobody can predict what happens across a lifetime. And sure, some of what happens might be unexpected tragedy, illness and suffering. Having chosen to live past the angst of adolescence, I've had my share of all of these. When I returned to dance classes in my fifties I expected to be unfit and stiff. What I didn't expect was that post chemotherapy and two years of medical treatment in my late fifties, the excellent balance I'd always taken for granted was completely shot. I could have walked unsteadily away, hung up my dance shoes for the final time. Instead, I hung in there and inched my way back, regaining the balance I had once taken for granted. Turns out flexibility of mind counts far more than flexibility of body.

To the young ones who currently despair of themselves: your dreams are not stillborn; they are waiting for you to breathe them into life. Make the choice to live. It does not mean you will escape pain and struggle; it is likely you will still have seasons of depression. But live. Because from that single choice springs the possibility of so many tiny miracles unimaginable from your current frame of mind. And they don't stop at 30 or 40 or 50 years of age. If anything, they seem to have accelerated since I entered my sixties. I now fully expect them to continue as long as I do. I wish the same for you.

To live is the rarest thing in the world. Most people just exist.

OSCAR WILDE

A HUNTER'S SPIRIT

Philip Erwin

Dad sat in his wheelchair, elbows on the padded arms, bony hands clasped loosely over his chest. Crystal-blue eyes scanning the hillside behind the house, slowly tracking to the left, then to the right. Left, then right. Up toward the summit; back down to the base, and left again. Then right.

Dad was hunting.

He hunted with his eyes.

He pursed his lips and whistled, at once plaintive and beseeching, the notes making a musical query: *Where-where-where-ARE-youuuu? Where-ARE-youuu?* The piercing, haunting call of the California valley quail. *Where-ARE-youuuu?* Dad whistled. Three notes, the second a third interval higher than the first, the third note starting just below the first, sliding down one note, two, three, like a jazz trumpeter milking the slide, squeezing out emotion, giving out on air. Then back again to the first note to repeat the question: *Where-where-where-ARE-youuuu? Where-ARE-youuu?*

Dad was hunting quail with his ears.

And the quail obliged him, clucking tentatively, then answering with a single shrill whistle: *Up-up-up-up-HERE!! Up-up-up-HEEERE!!!*

Dad's eyes swept to the right, up the hill, focusing, pinpointing the hummock, the very bush from which the shrill answer had come. *There! Under the manzanita! In the deep shadows ... six heads bobbing, a mamma quail and her five chicks!*

Dad repeated his call, and mamma quail answered. A conversation ensued, like a question-and-answer session in a church congregation:

Where-where-where-ARE-youuuu? Where-ARE-youuu?

Up-up-up-up-up-HEEERE!!! Up-up-HEEERE!!!

And mamma quail grew calm, trusting now that a papa quail was calling her from further down the hill. And she led her chicks out into the late afternoon sunlight, led them out away from the safety of the shrubs, out onto the flat, where the low grasses barely covered the little bodies of the baby quail. We could see their heads bobbing in frantic rhythms as they rushed across the grass, down the slope, seeking more shelter and whatever food was awaiting them at the bottom of the hill.

Dad sat motionless, watching. Only his blue eyes moved.

One hundred and one years old. Wheelchair-bound, body a slight shade of the stocky outdoorsman that had hiked and hunted mountains in twelve states and four continents; face lined with the weather of a hundred summers spent outdoors, picking peaches in youth, building mountain roads as a young man, building homes and surveying land for a living. Hunting and fishing only on vacations in later years, remembering his youth, paying homage to it: growing up on the foothill slopes of the Sierra Nevada, taking pack trips to the back country for weeks at a time, fishing through the summers, hunting through fall.

One hundred years of life's efforts and challenges pressing him down into that chair, squeezing the vigour out of his body, making both of us aware of just how fleeting a hundred years can be. But the hunter sat as quiet and still as ever, only the eyes moving, seeking, finding.

Hunting is about patience, and focus. Dad was the best hunter I ever knew.

He was a true California son, the youngest boy of a pioneer homesteader. He lived and worked and grew old in California's suburbs, but his spirit never left the chaparral slopes of the Sierra hill country, and the granite peaks that stood behind. 'I've seen mountains all over the world,' he would remind me, sitting above a whispering creek on family vacations, with our lines dangling in quiet currents. 'These are the best mountains anywhere.'

And he had seen mountains everywhere. Trips up into Canada in his youth; exploring the Sierra Madre south of Mexico with his mining-engineer brother. In North Africa, when Rommel was charging his tanks around the sands, Dad was a civilian contractor working high up in Eritrea to keep Allied aircraft flying against the Italian and German forces, as well servicing aircraft used in the famed pan-Himalaya 'hump route'.

'Servicing aircraft' didn't just mean keeping them running. It meant cleaning out the blood and bits of bone and tissue when they limped back in from a bad run.

There wasn't much game up on the plateau where the base was located, so he and his pals hopped on jeeps and descended 7000 feet to the lowlands to hunt wild pig and antelope. But when Rommel was defeated and the Africa contract wound down, Dad's ship took him home by way of Australia and New Zealand, where he was impressed by the crags that could be seen south of Wellington. He always regretted not having stayed behind to explore.

Back in California, he barely had time to wash his clothes before he was drafted into the army. They sent him to the South for training, and he travelled by rail through the mountains of Kentucky, Tennessee and Alabama before being stationed in the lowlands of Mississippi. You might think there wasn't much hunting on an army base, but a Southern belle caught and held his hunter's eye.

'Patience, my boy,' Dad often remarked to me. 'It takes patience to spot game. Patience, and focus. That's how you bring home worthwhile trophies.'

In Mississippi, his hunter's patience proved invaluable. He brought home to California a wife who loved him unfailingly for 64 years.

As we sat that late afternoon, watching the quail run down the hill to their evening meal, I thought perhaps Dad was caught up in reminiscing about his youthful outdoors life. The hill behind our house was covered with sage, manzanita, grasses and scrub oak, just like the hills where his father had homesteaded. I thought Dad must be lost in reverie, reliving his wonderfully wild youth.

'What are you thinking, Dad?' I asked, quietly, so as not to spook the quail.

He was quiet long enough I was beginning to wonder if he'd heard me. Those ears, after all, were almost 102 years old. But they still worked.

He was just patiently focusing on the question, seeking a trophy answer. And when it came, it surprised me.

'I was thinking,' he said, unclasping his hands and gesturing wide. 'I wonder what comes next.'

I didn't understand at first, and said so.

'Well,' he said, sounding just a bit like Reagan. 'I've lived a lot of years. And they've mostly been good years. I can't complain, I've seen a lot, I've done a lot. Been given a lot. And I've been alive to see some amazing changes in the world. I remember the first time I saw an automobile. My first time in an airplane. I was alive when men could not yet fly, and yet was able to watch when they flew to the moon. We used pencil and paper to do our writing and our figuring, and now nobody needs those any more, they can do everything on a computer. When I went from Africa to San Francisco, it took six weeks on the water; now it might be six days. Everything is so much better now, so much faster … It's really amazing how things change. So I was just thinking: I wonder what the next hundred years will bring?

'It's a lot of bother, getting so old, but I can't complain about it. I've had such a satisfying life, I can't feel sorry for myself. But if there's one thing I regret, it's that I won't be around to see what comes next. What the next hundred years will bring.'

The spirit of a true hunter. Eyes always scanning the distance, patiently waiting to see what trophies life will bring into view.

Nothing is more beautiful than the smile that has struggled through the **tears**.

DEMI LOVATO

ROMEO AND JULIET

Barbara Ascoli

I thought she was more resilient, this young granddaughter of mine. She had survived a year of bullying in her class from a boy who had become fixated on her with her angel face and blonde hair.

Her mother and I thought we had done all we could to support her, but we hadn't. We encouraged her with strategies to work around the bully such as how to deal with his demands; and how to avoid him. Her mother also met with school teachers. Some negotiation skills and other strategies worked for a short time. But that bully was a bright kid and he was the one with the power. The power to control this younger child and to hover over her constantly at lunch breaks and demand that she stay with him.

She told me one day she said to him, 'I'll play with you today at recess but I want to play with my friends at lunch time.'

That did not work. When he harassed her again, she asked a teacher for help and was told, 'Just go play with him. He likes you.'

I understand busy teachers. I value their roles. But there are some not doing their jobs. They are not always protecting our children when we pass them into their care. The bully was well known in the school but because my grandchild was kind to him she was often used as a tool by her teacher to help control this uncontrollable bully.

'Why do you sit next to him?' I asked.

'I don't. Wherever we sit in groups he just pushes in and sits next to me. The teacher lets him stay next to me. He starts talking, even in meditation, and I have to say "shush" to him to try to keep him quiet.'

Why did this bully continue to harass my grandchild over many months and push her friends away? I know now one of the main factors was an incompetent teacher. A teacher who was non-observant and didn't see what was happening in front of him. A teacher whose contract was not renewed at the end of the year. A teacher whose classroom was finally trashed by the bully because my grandchild finally said 'no' to one of the bully's requests. A classroom evacuated due to the violence of one powerful child.

'What did you do when he was throwing the chairs?' I asked her.

'I was hiding behind the concrete column where sometimes he doesn't see me.'

'Didn't any other teachers hear the commotion?'

'One looked in. Maybe she got the principal because he came in later.'

What had my grandchild said 'no' to? It was a 'no' to being Juliet in Shakespeare's *Romeo and Juliet*. The bully was the producer, the director, and in the starring role of Romeo. I knew my grandchild was anxious in preparing for the role of Juliet but I thought the play was being supervised by the drama or classroom teacher, not by a new producer on the block.

'We have to nail it by lunchtime,' she told me the day before the final show.

Nailed alright. She was crucified. Watched by the crowd.

Romeo finally left town. Juliet left bruised and traumatized.

Why didn't I ask more questions as that bullying progressed over many months? I now know. Listen. Listen. Listen is the key. We have now heard the full story, and worse than the final *Romeo and Juliet* incident we've heard about all the overt bullying that was going on for many months, and continued the following year, in that toxic environment.

How could this kind, gentle child be so isolated from her friendship groups? I've now seen that when bullying is left to flourish and continue without any discipline, then that community develops more types of bullying (including covert bullying). This covert bullying seems to be often hidden from or ignored by teachers. It is the snide remarks, the putting down, the taunting, the isolating, the starting of rumours, and the many other ways to highlight a child's different characteristics. This can be a bullying minefield with the bombs hidden from view, but some know very well where those bombs are planted to cause most harm.

My grandchild is small and beautiful. She embraces this saying, 'I love tiny things. Tiny animals. Tiny houses. Tiny people.'

After her dramatic year she said, 'I did not like always having to stand under my classmates' smelly armpits so they could see how small I am.'

In our family we teach non-violence but there are times when this nana could rage.

I hear more stories.

'You know how you told me to help someone else if I'm feeling sad or have no friends around? Well at lunchtime, I saw this little kindergarten kid by herself and I went to play with her but my friends took my lunchbox to the bin so I had to rush back and get it. Then they ran away.

'And the other day I was by myself at recess and I saw this beautiful tree. I thought I'd have that tree as a friend, like *Anne of Green Gables*. Afterwards I saw … and thought I'd tell her about my new friend. Well, she went straight away to the others and they all ran to the tree and wrecked it. They tore off all the leaves and the bark. I cried for that tree.'

These stories sound like small incidents, but it is the consistency of these and similar stories that is so painful. All children, at times, will tease or make fun of others, and we have to teach our children to take some of these taunts. We all get teased, as children and adults, and we can learn different ways of dealing with occasional taunts. But constant teasing and isolating a child because that child is somehow different from the wider group is just plain wrong.

I heard more stories of covert bullying from my grandchild but only after she became ill. She was not sleeping or eating properly, unable to concentrate and extremely sad.

'I've just kept it in for so long,' she said. 'I have no friends.'

'You are a child, not an adult, you do not have to deal with this yourself,' I answered.

My grandchild did have some good communication skills but she was left unsupported by her so-called 'school friends'. These were friends who had frequently visited our home for plays, meals and parties. Many of the children in my granddaughter's class may have looked at their classmates and thought, *It's okay if we tease ... as everyone does it and no one has told us to stop. We're not bullies. We are just having a bit of fun. Mum and Dad are not worried about it.*

If we had heard about the incidents of overt bullying we would have approached the school earlier. We were late in doing this, but the school was also too late in observing what was happening in their classrooms and playgrounds. And when they were informed they did too little too late.

What I've learnt from this experience is that individual strategies will not always help the child with bullying. At times I wish I was a 'helicopter' grandparent, constantly hovering over my grandchildren and protecting them by intervening at the smallest mishap. But I have a strong belief that children can work through many difficulties themselves and grow through this into mature and caring adults. As parents and grandparents we have to give our children space to grow. But our society and culture is changing — the focus is now on power and wealth and personal achievement at all costs. Kind, good, caring people are not always valued. I believe my grandchild was bullied because she was that kind child with a strong belief in helping others. She was not into power or possession.

At her new school she had the courage to talk to her classmates about how she had been bullied. We all learnt from this.

The other day she said, 'I love my new school and new friends. Look at my certificate, "for being pure sunshine and bringing positivity to our classroom every day".'

How sweet is love not possessed?

Well done, Juliet.

The way to get started is to quit talking and **begin** doing.

WALT DISNEY

A DREAM THAT CAME TRUE

Joan Levy Earle

Ask most writers and they will tell you (if they answer honestly) that their dream is to hear someone say: 'Yes, we will publish this.'

I had the same dream. I was married to a man who told one of my friends on New Year's Eve, 2003: 'You know, Joan is a pretty good writer.' Five days later, I found my husband Jack Earle's body lying outside on a cold January day. He had succumbed to a fatal heart attack at 61.

Jack had seemed to be in good health. He liked to do a daily run and to cross-country ski, so many of his male friends were shocked by his passing. At his wake they said: 'Jack went the way we want to go; he died with his boots on.'

We had purchased an old farm property and Jack had been living there without power or water for three years. I was operating our family bookstore and visiting with him for weekends. At the time of his death, I had just moved to be permanently with him at the farm; the bookstore had been closed and the building sold. We sipped champagne that weekend and celebrated our good fortune because the funds were now in the bank to finish the house renovations, and we were about to begin the rest of our lives together.

When he died, I became a student of living on one's own in the country. I had never put a log in a wood stove before and had not driven a car for 30 years. Good friends helped, and in that first year I began keeping a more serious journal of notes about life as a widow, and also memories of life with an amazingly independent man named Jack.

About nine months after his passing, our son John had finished the wiring of the farmhouse, applied for the necessary approval and with the funds from the sale of our downtown building, power arrived at the 100-year-old structure that had been Jack's dream project. He had completed the bull work: new sub-floors, new windows, new drywall upstairs. He had even given me a special gift of a library by taking out the third bedroom. When you climbed up the stairs you were flooded with the sunlight from three windows. Everyone marvelled at the sturdy shelves, now stacked with hundreds of my favourite volumes. Jack loved reading too, and some of his friends inherited his solar power installation books; one of his goals had been to live off the grid. Without him to maintain the solar power system, I had no choice but to accept the more conventional system of 'power on poles' from the nearest connection, a quarter of a mile away. Thousands of dollars later, I was able to dispense with our single propane Humphrey lamp, and flip a switch whenever twilight surrounded the house.

For several months, I had been writing articles about Jack and his life in the country, which I had hoped to sell to a country magazine. One day Jack gave me a title: *The House That Time Forgot*. That title inspired me to take some of the ideas in those articles and begin writing a book about Jack and his renovation project. With the convenience of power, I could now use a computer and, sitting at my desk in the newly built library, surveying the hundred acres of forest and quiet that surrounded me, I had peace in my heart that despite my loss of a husband, it had truly been a blessing to have been married to him for 36 years.

Within a few months, and after much disciplined effort, I had a manuscript, loosely titled: *The House That Time Forgot*. One day just before Christmas and the approaching first anniversary of Jack's death, I decided to make a phone call to a small regional publisher. Although she had rejected two other manuscripts of mine over the last few years, I respected her opinion. She had been very kind in her critique of my writing, sending a full-page letter to explain why she was rejecting each manuscript. I had responded with my own letter of appreciation for her encouragement.

When I called her office that day, she recognized my name and inquired about my life. I told her of my husband's sudden death, and also that I had just written about Jack's dream of owning this secluded property in the middle of nowhere. She seemed curious, and despite having a desk full of manuscripts she asked me to send the finished manuscript to her.

I spent the next few days polishing the manuscript and off it went. The publisher contacted me again about a month later and said that she had read it one Sunday morning, and could not put it down. She liked it but wasn't yet saying that she would be publishing it. She wanted more details about opportunities and suggestions I might have for helping with the marketing, which was to be expected in the competitive world of publishing.

The next time she phoned it was late in the afternoon. She told me that she had made a decision. Yes, she just had to publish this book but wanted to change the name to *Jack's Farm*. I had no problem with that.

She said she considered it a love story about Jack's love for the land, the outdoors, and for me. I think my heart skipped a beat when I said to her: 'Do you know what day this is?' She had been so busy that she had forgotten that the date was 14 February, Valentine's Day.

One year later, by courier, a beautiful hardbound book arrived at my door. The dust jacket bore the photo of the farm's laneway with its impressive trees on either side. I had self-published eight other books, and now, at last, I was going to live my dream of being published by a commercial publisher.

There is no doubt in my mind that a certain man named Jack may have whispered in her heart from heaven: 'Give Joan a little gift from me today.'

People who succeed have momentum. The more they succeed, the more they want to succeed, and the more they find a way to succeed. Similarly, when someone is failing, the tendency is to get on a downward spiral that can even become a self-fulfilling prophecy.

TONY ROBBINS

THE OLDEST KID IN
MEDICAL SCHOOL

Carol Scot

In 1945, when I was ten years old, I learnt — from a library book — that there were doctors for the mind called psychologists and psychiatrists, named after the goddess Psyche. That sounded worthy and interesting, so I decided I would become a mind doctor when I grew up.

What an embarrassing joke on me! By age twelve I had been made to understand that girls couldn't be doctors; their proper and joyful lives were to be love, marriage and having babies.

I started early on that womanly mission, falling in love with a younger high school classmate, Ron, and soon, in 1953, having our first daughter. By the time I was 25 we had four daughters and I'd had a tubal ligation to keep from having more.

In 1967 Ron completed a Master's degree and advanced from teaching high school to teaching at Auburn Community College in upstate New York. I'd been working as a computer programmer for several years, and was also hired by ACC to work in their data centre. As a staff member I could take courses, so in the time I worked there I was able, in 1970, to get an Associate of Arts degree.

That same year I didn't get a renewal contract. No explanation, but apparently Ron and I had had some arguments on campus, and someone had to be punished. He had tenure, giving him job security, so it had to be me.

Our marriage was strained because for eight or nine years Ron had had outside interests, and he started another, spending quite a bit of time with his female office mate. I became despairing, even suicidal, but I hung on, never acting on those feelings because I didn't want my children to have to live with such a trauma. But I really needed not to be around him and Her, so with his agreement I went to Washington DC where an aunt and uncle lived, to see about continuing my education.

I took a position as a live-in children's maid caring for William Safire's son and daughter, aged six and five. On my days off I investigated colleges. American University said they would credit my AA degree for its two years of work, and give me a Returning Housewife scholarship. With that and the burgeoning women's liberation movement, my dream of becoming a doctor began to feel possible.

But on a visit home I realized Ron wasn't doing as good a job of single parenting as I had thought he would, so I put the dream on hold and went home to the kids instead.

Ron and I were divorced in 1971. For the break-up I had a lawyer, but somehow I was divorced without being at the event. I was just told it had been accomplished, and since it was obvious I could support myself, I received no alimony. Ron paid only paltry child support.

I looked for work, applying for all sorts of things. I worked a few months as the maid at a boarding house before I got another programming job with a manufacturing company.

By 1973 our three oldest girls had finished high school and were off to college. Ron had married the office mate and they were willing, even eager, to have our youngest daughter live with them, so I was freed to pick up my education.

We sold our home, and I started the third year of college at the American University (AU) in Washington DC, staying for a while with my aunt and uncle and then taking another live-in childcare position. By then I was 38 years old. Reading information on what medical schools required and the statistics on admissions — only 8 per cent of applicants over the age of 30 were admitted the previous year — once again made me wonder whether I could do it.

For both my AA and Bachelor degrees, I saved time and money by taking proficiency exams, mostly in non-scientific required courses. While working and taking care of the girls I could not take any science courses at night, because those courses required two evenings a week for lecture and laboratory.

I entered AU planning to become a psychologist rather than a physician. Into my second year of successful courses in psychology, statistics and other subjects, I thought I should start getting advice about applying to graduate school. I went to one after another of the psych professors attempting to find help. Instead I received discouragement. One advised me to find employment in the psychology field by getting a Master's degree in testing. Their attitude was, 'Of course you want to be a clinical psychologist. Everybody wants to be a clinical psychologist.'

But I was set on doctorhood. My attitude was, 'I'll go anywhere. Surely there's a school that will take me. I'll go to South Dakota if I have to.'

The final professor I talked to, in trying to convince me it was hopeless, said in exasperation, 'We get hundreds of applications for our ten positions here. It's as hard to get into clinical psychology as it is to get into medical school.'

Hmm.

I reviewed the application requirements for medical school again. I already had calculus and physics from my first two years at ACC. And because I'd felt that even as a psychologist I should know something about the physical bodies my patients lived in, I'd taken and passed the proficiency course for the first semester of biology, and then took the second semester of biology. My assigned laboratory partner was a young man, a pre-med student. When we were cutting up the foetal pig, I became so excited about the marvel of the anatomy of its intestines — how magically they were constructed, how efficiently packed in with the beautiful arcade of blood vessels supplying them, and their ability to adjust size and position to do their work — that my partner said, 'You're the one who should be going to medical school.'

All I lacked to be able to apply to medical school were a year of chemistry and one of organic chemistry. Two more years?

To try to make it shorter, I signed up and took the chemistry proficiency exam, and tried to sign up to take organic chemistry in its ten-week summer course. But I was told I couldn't sign up for organic chemistry because I didn't have the prerequisite chemistry course on my record. It wouldn't appear until I received my test score, which would be too late to register for and start the summer course.

I requested a meeting with the head of the department. In his office I asked him whom it would hurt if I failed the proficiency test and/or failed the summer course. He agreed it would hurt only me, overrode the restriction, and let me take the risk.

Wasn't he wonderful!

So I began organic chemistry, not knowing whether taking it would be an exercise in futility.

The first five weeks of summer school covered the first semester of organic chemistry. We had a delightful woman professor whose beginning words to us were, 'Oh, you poor people. You're not going to be doing anything this summer but chemistry. No social life. No trips to the beach. Just work. Just chemistry.'

But she also said that organic chemistry was basically a cooking class, learning how chemical ingredients came together to create new substances. That helped me through the weeks of daily lectures and labs.

I had also obtained a government programming job, which I did in the evenings, riding a bus to a building downtown. That income let me rent a two-room apartment near AU, close enough to walk to classes instead of having to drive.

I passed the chemistry proficiency test, barely, and received an A in lecture and a B in laboratory for the organic chemistry course.

Now I could apply to medical schools.

Each application cost $30, so I could afford only ten. My rejection from Duke came fast. They cashed my cheque and said they did not accept applications from persons older than 30.

Out of the ten, four invited me for interviews: the University of Kentucky in Lexington, George Washington in DC, Tufts in Boston, and Albert Einstein in New York City.

At Albert Einstein, an interviewer must have disagreed with the decision to invite me. He asked me, 'How can you justify taking up a place in medical school at your age?'

I'd heard that question in my nightmares and had an answer. 'Because I'll still be practising when my male classmates have kicked off from heart attacks or accidents.' No admission from AE, but yes from the others.

As a 42-year-old third-year medical student in Kentucky, working at 3 a.m., I was flooded with the knowledge I was in exactly the right place, doing exactly what I wanted.

And as an 83-year-old physician now, still licensed and practising, I say all the struggle was worth it.

Only in the
darkness can
you see the stars.

MARTIN LUTHER KING JR

MIRRORS: A MEMOIR

Gayle Malloy

When a mirror shatters, there is always some part of it that is lost forever. It may just be a residue of fine dust, perhaps a tiny shard, but whatever it is, it is irretrievable. My life became a shattered mirror. I picked up the pieces, glued them back as best I could, but what I had was forever lost.

New Year's Eve, 1971, and Western Australia sweltered in the summer's relentless heat. Waking to the clatter of trolleys, unidentifiable smells and the hum of air conditioning, I looked around to see an empty room painted puke green. Lying in a clean white hospital bed, my body aching and my arm encased in plaster, I raised my hand to my cheek to feel not the softness of flesh but the coarseness of a bandage supporting my jaw. Something had happened to me, but I couldn't remember what.

A young nurse entered the room, asked if I felt strong enough to stand up and before I had a chance to mumble my reply expertly tugged me out of the hospital bed. Together we shuffled down the corridor towards the shower stalls, where the air was heavy with moisture.

On the wall hung a mirror speckled with pearls of wetness, the droplets forming tiny streams cascading towards the floor. Breathing in the pungent odour of antiseptic soap, I stumbled past the bathroom mirror and glanced at my reflection. Trapped within the mirror's silver bars, a monster looked back at me, a startled expression on its face. In horror I looked at its red swollen flesh with black train tracks of stitching crisscrossing its cheeks, lips, nose, eyelids and forehead. Surely the lights and the moisture were distorting the image in the mirror. Reaching out, I rubbed the moisture away, but no, the image remained. Through slitted eyes it looked back at me, then lifting its chin it showed me its left cheek where a slash from ear to mouth made it look as if some demonic being had tried to decapitate it. Its mutilated features were warped into two alien half-faces, the left pulling down with the slashing of the cheek and mouth, the right pulling upwards as the nose, eyebrow and forehead had been sliced. Reaching up with my right hand I traced the black train tracks of stitches on my face. My fingertips pressed against the rigid black threads then travelled down to my swollen lips where I felt the hard knob of windscreen glass embedded underneath the skin. Sometime in the last 24 hours I had become the creature in the mirror.

Nearly 50 years later and that moment is still etched in my psyche in a visceral, somatic response. Every time I look in a mirror, for a fleeting moment I relive the despair of that day.

I no longer blush when someone looks at me but I can remember the moment when it all started. My first visit to the outpatient clinic, again the puke green walls, the unidentifiable smells, but this time sitting quietly, making minimal eye contact. My jaw was broken on both sides and due to the slicing of my face could not be wired, so a bandage kept it in place and also hid my facial wounding. The other outpatients gave me a few suspicious glances, but they were too wrapped up in their own misery to really notice me. Everyone had been given the same appointment time. The clinic was at full capacity. My name was called and I arose and walked towards the doctor's office. The doctor, a man in his mid thirties, checked my name off his list and standing in front of his office door looked at the bandage. He started to unwind it. My heart beat faster, I held my breath. My mind screamed, *Not here, not in front of all these people.* The doctor continued to unwrap the bandaging. I glanced towards the captive audience of outpatients to this, my unveiling. A few grimaced, a small child pointed and asked, 'What's that on her face?' Others just stared out of curiosity. The drama being played out in front of them acted as a diversion to their bored waiting. The doctor gave a cursory glance at the wounding. Just a glance, in front of his office, before an audience of bored outpatients. I had been devalued to a quick glance in front of a room full of strangers. I felt the warmth of a blush creep across my face. I had never blushed before, but the humiliation of the unveiling triggered a response in my body. It screamed its misery in the only way it could, by blushing. Through adolescence and early adulthood I blushed whenever anyone looked at me.

What do I see reflected within the mirror's silver bars now that I am 64? The eighteen-year-old's startled expression is forever frozen in time. She still peers back, I still feel the sadness, but only for a moment. The image soon morphs into a mature face with skin that has lost its elasticity, so that the scar that sat so prominently on my cheek, now resides on my sagging jaw line. I may see myself as disfigured and dispossessed, no longer a part of the greater tribe, but there is a place for me in the world. My scarring gave me a depth of understanding that allowed me to work with the broken, the downtrodden and the dispossessed. I can meet them halfway; they can see just by looking at me that I am a fellow traveller. The prism through which we view the world is different from those who have not experienced hardship. As their counsellor I journey with them to a better life, showing them how to cope with life's rejections and helping them to find the jewels in each moment.

The struggles of overcoming facial disfigurement rewarded me with the gift of compassion and understanding of 'the other'. It allowed me to journey down a different path and to experience the success of helping others create a better life. Without the scarring I don't know who I would be.

Everyone you meet is fighting a battle you know nothing about. **Be kind.** Always!

ROBIN WILLIAMS

MANIC RIDE

Kim Beatrice

It was a time when wolf whistles and bum patting weren't frowned upon and I cycled Lower Hutt streets delivering mail for the *Post & Telegraph*, now *New Zealand Post*. There was camaraderie amongst outdoor workers, from council workers to traffic cops and police officers. The council boys, if I was fast enough, would give me a ride up my steepest hill on the back of the rubbish truck. The discarded waste, blowflies and the stench never bothered me — the walk up the hill did, and I made sure I was never late. As the truck crawled up the hill and the boys stood on the back step, I rearranged my mail, my legs dangling comfortably. At the top we'd jump off and begin the downhill race, the driver laughing at us. But our jobs got done, rubbish collected and mail delivered to pretty homes with manicured gardens.

Then the good times ended. A hidden crisis lurked within and my health deteriorated. I couldn't handle the most basic tasks. My brain was shutting down. I tried to ignore the obvious but finally had to take sick leave. Unbeknown to me, I was suffering from acute manic depression. Struggling to cope with this drastic change and not understanding what was happening to me, I made five suicide attempts.

Those closest to me could see nothing wrong, no blood, cuts, bruises or breaks. As my mental health worsened, I was hospitalized in the care of a wonderful psychiatric support team. Our first group discussion was about mental illness being invisible and people's reactions because they couldn't see an injury. It was an illuminating discussion and afterwards, jokingly, we were all offered a plaster for our foreheads. My family couldn't accept my illness, but welfare officers from the post office visited me, bringing fruit and kindness. My supervisor came often, and she was like my guardian angel, bringing light and warmth into the room.

A year later I left the hospital, entering a confusing and uncertain world. On occasion I would stagger like a drunk, unable to talk. Those around me were solicitous, but that made me feel under scrutiny and broken. At home, I would stare at the letterbox, unable to get there to collect the mail. I agonized about how to get to the bank. I became so frail I couldn't walk properly. My mother would take me shopping, but in most shops I had to sit down, either sit or fall over. The doctors adjusted my medication until my slow, faltering journey back to normality began.

I left New Zealand in the mid 1980s and spent 25 years in Australia, initially as a single mum. I didn't qualify for a single mothers' benefit, but with a little girl who needed food in her belly and clothes on her back, I learnt how to build houses and brick walls, lay lawns, cook, sort letters, and once gave myself in lieu of payment, for supplies to make jewellery that I could sell at local markets.

Leaving New Zealand was the crucial first step in recuperating from my disease, known today as bipolar disorder. I settled in Australia, facing my illness head-on. Some days I couldn't go out unless I recited nursery rhymes silently to myself. Other days I still stumbled like a drunk because of my medication's side effects. A year into living in Australia, my health began to deteriorate again and I had to do the single hardest thing of my life: send my daughter back to her father in New Zealand while I recovered. I was dreadfully lonely without her, but I had to get well and become strong before she could come back to me.

As I spiralled back into illness, I began drinking excessively, which magnified my side effects and mood swings. Some days I was untouchable; I could walk on water. Other days I couldn't leave my flat. When I was up I could do three jobs a day. There were one-night stands and gambling on the pokies. When I was down I would stay in bed in my small flat in the middle of Surfers Paradise for days. I knew I had to get a grip, and my first step was to stop drinking. In my lonely hours, I started fiddling around with poetry and began a small course in writing for children. Writing helped me focus, laughing at my own stories and shedding tears as I faced up to reality. It was a tough time but I survived it, and two years later my beautiful daughter was back in my arms again smiling and giggling. Our fretting for one another had ended. Our happiness was complete. My daughter gave me strength and purpose, and with the help of my psychiatrists I adjusted to my disability, finally accepting the fact that I had a permanent mental illness.

At about this time, my daughter's father and I divorced. Fortunately for all three of us, it was amicable. He and I married young and had drifted apart (my illness didn't help). I met him again at our daughter's wedding, and he is still a good person. I married again twice in Australia. My second husband needed to be by himself with his bottles. My third, a gentle, kind and caring person, listened and cried with me when I told him my stories. He loved and held me close and still does.

My health seemed stable, so I decided to go back to school, enrolling at Griffith University on the Gold Coast in Queensland as a mature student. Three years later, I graduated with a BA in creative arts. After I graduated, my husband's work took us to Tasmania, and I went to the University of Tasmania, receiving an English degree with honours. Unexpectedly, I suffered another setback. I remember the day when I handed a paper in to my lecturer. He asked me what it was. I looked at him fearfully, shaking my finger at it as if to say 'Well go on … You read it.' I left his office, closed the door, and I truly could have fallen straight on my face that day.

I'd thought I was cured and had foolishly stopped taking my medication. I was not responding to tasks again and went to my doctor to renew my prescription. I gave him my information, but he insisted that my psychiatrist had to be involved before he would give me anything. I asked him to telephone her, but he refused. He yelled at me, so I yelled back at him. I never saw him again. I rang my psychiatrist in Queensland and told her what happened. She express-posted my medical notes to a new doctor I'd found. It took several visits and weekly blood tests to get the dosage right before my health slowly improved.

My husband's job took us back to Queensland, and by this time I was well again, back to doing those mundane things a wife and mother does. Settled back in Queensland, I completed two creative writing Master's degrees at the University of Canberra and from Deakin University online.

Then my brother rang me to come home — Mum was dying. I rushed home to her finger shaking at a hospice booklet and the list of medication she had to take. I bawled my eyes out while she talked as if nothing was wrong, her soft voice telling me, 'Don't cry.' Mum's health failed rapidly, and inside a week her words were unintelligible and she could barely sit up. I talked to my husband in Australia every day, and he convinced my daughter, who was struggling to cope with her nanna passing, to telephone her. Mum was resting when she called. At the sound of her granddaughter's voice, Mum's eyes opened wide and she sat straight up, but sadly, her words were garbled and unintelligible. Her medicine stopped working, my fishcakes (which she loved) went untouched, and I knew her time was near. She passed peacefully in her sleep two days later. Ferns lined her grave at the family plot, and we sang Māori songs while the pallbearers lowered her coffin. She knew I was okay before she passed, but most importantly, I got to say goodbye when Mum was bright and lucid enough for me to do it. Her passing broke the last link to my previous life.

I'm retired now — 36 years into my illness, living in rural Manawatu. I have been stable for many years now, religiously taking my tablets and regular blood tests so I don't relapse. I forget I have the illness, although a wobble every now and then reminds me, but I just sleep it off. I'm even thinking about doing a PhD in creative writing — I can feel my mum still around me. She will be proud.

I failed my way
to success.

THOMAS EDISON

CALIGULA

Roger Chapman

I don't understand machines. Nor did my father — he couldn't tell a gasket from a gantry. But unlike him, I no longer expect machines to behave predictably — they're more like humans, indulging their passions at whim.

The dishwasher is especially ill-tempered. Understandable, perhaps — washing up is tedious, and there's no evident reason why a machine should enjoy it. Some may say it's merely venting its spleen. But the dishwasher is more calculating than that. Like most of us, it cherishes the comfort of a snug, warm home, and for that reason avoids breaking down completely — which would, as it's obviously figured out, lead to its banishment. No, it creates just enough mischief to demand whatever attention will restore it to full working order, free to harass me again when it's ready.

Not only do I have to tolerate its malevolence — I'm helpless when something goes wrong. Just mention the words 'instruction manual' and my knees start to quiver. My mouth goes dry and sweat bedews my forehead. Many men are happy to spend hours wielding tools underneath cars, or mending clocks. Not me. When I try repairing a broken artefact, I'm left with an assortment of gears, springs and flywheels which defy re-insertion. And it's still broken.

Instruction manuals have a section headed 'Troubleshooting', which makes fixing the problem sound manly and efficient. But they contain only anodyne suggestions such as 'Ensure the device is plugged into a power outlet' and 'Switch the power on' — steps that even I can think of unaided. And there's nothing about the precise predicament that faces me. It's as if the manufacturer was unable to conceive that the appliance might malfunction in this particular way, and thus saw no need to suggest a remedy.

So I no longer meddle; I send for an expert. Even this is fraught with apprehension — I know he (it's never a woman) will pity me, and sneer inwardly at my cowardice and technical not-know-how. And when he diagnoses and cures the sickness, I'm left with the suspicion that, if I'd really tried, I could have done it.

Nineteen seventy-six. My wife and I, married seven years, have just moved to the Wellington suburb of Kelburn. In doing so, we've acquired a dishwasher. No matter that it's elderly, if not obsolete — it's our chance to put kitchen-sinkery behind us and begin a leisured after-dinner life. The machine will take over (though it's mildly disappointing to find it has no setting for emptying itself and putting the clean utensils away).

Below the lid there's a circular basket for arranging the dishes. In my ignorance, I wonder if it works like our washing machine: once you press the start button, the basket will begin to rotate, gathering momentum until the crockery and glasses within are shattered. It's a relief to find that my fears are groundless.

But the machine soon begins to falter and, after a short illness, it turns its dial to the wall and expires. Fortuitously, we're about to renovate the kitchen (and we've already grown used to the freedom from dishmops and detergents), so we order a shiny new one. I assume the suppliers will remove Old Unfaithful to some Elysian field for dead dishwashers, but I am much mistaken. They expect us to disconnect and dispose of it. I haven't the slightest inkling how to go about this, so my wife consults the salesman and duly reports the result.

'He says it's easy. You just take off the front of the dishwasher, turn off the tap inside, remove the wurgle, disconnect the spangling throcket and then unscrew the blodger. At least, I think that's what he said.'

The salesman, naturally unaware of the antipathy between my family and their machines, is seriously underestimating the danger. And I hardly feel competent to follow his instructions. I keep putting off any attempt until the arrival of the new dishwasher is imminent and then, against my better judgment, I set to work.

I genuflect before the machine. It might be wiser to use both knees and pray while I'm about it, but that never occurs to me. I intend my approach to be strictly practical, not spiritual. Astonishingly, I have no difficulty removing the front panel or turning off the tap, and — despite half-hearing a faint chortle from within — I proceed with slightly more confidence. But my comeuppance is at hand. A fine spray starts to leak from what I guess is the wurgle. The spray becomes a jet. My attempts to stem the flow by reversing the surgery I've just performed are, of course, completely unavailing. In no time, there's half an inch of warm water lapping round my shoes.

By the time Ollie the plumber arrives, a tepid lake has formed at one end of the kitchen (which, incidentally, is how I discover that the floor isn't level). He's relatively good-natured about my interrupting his Sunday lunch. I describe what I was attempting, but he merely gives me a pitying look. Ignoring the dishwasher, he advances on the hot water cylinder and turns off the tap. The cascade ceases.

'Didn't think of that,' I confess. I don't try to explain how foolish I feel.

'You shouldn't have tried this on your own,' he says.

Not that I need telling. 'Never again, that's for sure.'

In our next house, the dishwasher develops a leak all by itself, but is subtle enough to conceal it until our downstairs neighbour asks politely if we know why water is coming through her ceiling. After that we live in a rented apartment, whose resident dishwasher remains passive and uncomplaining — appreciating, no doubt, that it's the landlord, not me, who'll be paying for any repairs. The only leaks come through the ceiling and the walls when it rains.

The machine in our present home, however, has something to prove. Its innate viciousness is slow to emerge, and at first it's more or less compliant, if a little sullen. Then it tires of drying the dishes fully and develops a habit of leaving just enough residual moisture to wet the kitchen floor thoroughly when I empty it. After enjoying this for a bit, it gets bored and tries creating a more comprehensive flood. There's no advance warning, just a pond, accompanied by a smirk. Kevin the technician finds a hole in one of the hoses, caused (he says) by a rat dining at home. If this is his way of exonerating the dishwasher, I'm unconvinced. I think the dishwasher and the rat were in it together.

I begin to realize what I'm up against. The machine has a personality, and a vicious one at that. On the know-your-enemy principle I decide to give it a name — then I'll know better what to expect. The one that seems best suited to its brand of crazed malice is Caligula.

Caligula sulks under the kitchen bench, squirgling occasionally but otherwise merely exuding dumb insolence. After a while he decides to get trickier. One morning we find that he's decanted a trickle of water onto the floor. Not a flood this time, just enough to be annoying. After the trickle has reappeared several days in a row, I summon help. Kevin has left town, so I call Stan.

I should introduce the protagonists to each other — 'Caligula, I'd like you to meet Stan' — but I'm afraid of seeming paranoid. Stan says it's a simple problem: Caligula's door is not shutting fully and so isn't watertight. He fixes the door but, as we find a few hours later, not the leak. He's back the following day and after a few minutes announces that there was a minor problem with accumulated detergent scaling, which he has now removed. And nothing does leak out until just after the front door has closed behind him. Caligula is obviously making fun of us both, but at least I have an excuse.

I fire Stan and engage another technician. I'm relieved that Frank seems more knowledgeable. He explains that the leak had nothing to do with scaling; the looseness of the detergent dispenser is the seat of the problem. He de-loosens it, and pronounces the machine leak-free, which it proves to be for about an hour — the period which elapses before I decide to test it for myself. Back he comes next day; this time I think it best to stand over him while he works. He pulls Caligula out from under the bench and sets him going. That's when I notice a thin stream of water spurting from a hose at the back, forming a puddle on the floor.

'Could this have anything to do with it?' I ask timidly, not wanting to expose my ignorance. But when I see Caligula wince, I know I'm onto something.

'Well spotted. I should've picked that up.' Frank is gracious enough to look embarrassed. 'I'll soon fix it.' And within a few minutes the job's done.

I suspect that Caligula now knows who's in charge. He's on a warning that, if he misbehaves again, he'll be traded for a newer model. Since Frank left, there hasn't been a murmur from him. It would be foolhardy to assume yet that my problems are over, but I fancy that I may at least have begun to earn his respect. The world is looking a brighter place.

I should have known that Caligula wouldn't take kindly to being thwarted. Despite my giving him every chance, he couldn't keep up his act. In little ways, his frustration began to show. He left dishes — just a few — wet. The lights on his control panel flashed erratically. Finally, he overreached and went on strike altogether. I had no choice: I decommissioned him. Now, a sleek new number has taken his place. This one (her name is Gretchen, by the way) is quiet and efficient. You couldn't hope to meet a more accommodating or sweeter-tempered dishwasher.

But don't imagine that I'm going to allow her charm to lull me into lowering my guard. While I may have got the better of Caligula, there's no room for complacency. Oh no. And in case there's any further trouble, I'm just going to the shed to sharpen my spanner.

We are all broken,
that's how
the **light** gets in.

ERNEST HEMINGWAY

A WORK IN PROGRESS

Elizabeth Hansen

This morning I shared four very different videos on my Facebook page, and each one was important to me. I was on a roll!

The first was about a village in the Netherlands where dementia patients can wander freely and be safe. The patients were happy and consequently fewer carers were needed. What it meant to me is that when we create community, and have respect for the ageing, everyone benefits.

Then I shared a how-to video for making a bin liner out of newspaper, instead of using plastic bin liners. Plastic is choking the planet on the land and beaches and especially in the oceans. Caring for the environment, preserving forests and wildlife, has always been important to me, but now as I grow wiser, I understand there is no separation between us and the environment. We are all part of this one glorious organism that is our planet Earth. What harms the planet harms every one of us here, including all plant and animal life. Reversing the damage done by our excessive use of plastic can seem overwhelming, especially when the decisions are being made by faceless corporations, but every individual can make a difference. When enough of us make changes for the better, eventually we will reach the critical point where the tide turns. There is still hope if we all make an effort.

Next, a TED talk by Ken Robinson was about nurturing creativity in children by allowing them to make mistakes without fear. Picasso said creativity is in all children, and Ken encouraged seeing a child's creative capacity for the richness it is, and seeing children for the hope they are for the future. Our task is to educate the whole being without crushing the creativity.

The final video was a little boy singing a lullaby to his baby sister and he began to cry. He was crying because, he said, 'This is good, with Alice. It's so beautiful.' It was love that moved him to tears. Love, family and connection is beautiful.

So what does a diverse range of topics including care for the elderly, bin liners, creativity in education, and love have to say about me? About a decade ago I would have struggled to know what was important to me. I was consumed by busyness, working long days, and rarely taking time off. The additional demands of being wife, mother and homemaker left nothing for me. I realized this in a lightning bolt moment sitting in a conference when the speaker said, 'First it is essential to know yourself.'

Gradually, through the years of being who everyone else needed me to be, I had lost my sense of self. This was not an uncommon phenomenon for women at my stage of life at that time. In that moment, I made a commitment to try to rediscover me. Project 'Who am I?'

I knew that I enjoyed writing so I set myself the task of writing a book about my journey and decided to call it, not particularly imaginatively, *Know Yourself.*

I still haven't written that book. I started a number of times, getting quite a few chapters completed, but then life would take a whole new turn and show me I still had a lot more to learn on this journey of self-discovery.

Delete that document! Start again.

Like untangling a ball of wool after a kitten has wrestled it around the furniture, I was untangling the essence of me. One of my biggest u-turns on this journey happened when my marriage of more than three decades disintegrated. It was a shock to others as well as to me. We had been soulmates, I thought, but in recent times the relationship had become toxic, and I learnt that you really can't be certain of anything in life. For the first time I found myself living alone. What an opportunity to really get to know myself (although I don't recommend ending a marriage to do so; this is the silver lining in a sad situation).

What I began to notice is it's the little things that define who we are, like the groceries we put into our shopping trollies. I was used to shopping for the family, but now I could choose what I liked. It might seem easy but at times I was excited about these decisions, like red delicious apples instead of granny smiths, or cheesymite instead of vegemite. Seems crazy to some but it was like an epiphany to me.

It was around this time I started to meditate daily. This one change of habit set me on the path of a career change from a business owner to eventually teaching yoga and meditation instead. I was building a new network of friends and finding new ways to connect with my community. I attended an OM Fest mistakenly thinking it was about yoga, only to find it was an afternoon of Original Music by local musicians. It was a happy mistake because, consequently, I rediscovered my love of music and started playing the ukulele, poorly but with enthusiasm. I joined a choir, and I started to draw again.

I love being outside and find joy in sunrises, walking with my dog on the beach, and watching the birds that visit the lake near my home. These are all small things, but they define me in a way that is different to what I expected when I took the first wobbly steps of writing a book to find out who I was.

On my journey, I have learnt to be a better listener.

When we share a post on Facebook, it isn't just because we want to show it to our friends. It is more than that. We are calling out to connect with anyone who shares the same values. If they are listening, they respond. If we listen to our friends, we know and grow with them, too.

I still haven't finished writing that book, partly because I am still on my own journey. Perhaps I will be ready one day to send it out into the wide world of literature, but first I need to know myself, and that, my dear reader, is still a work in progress.

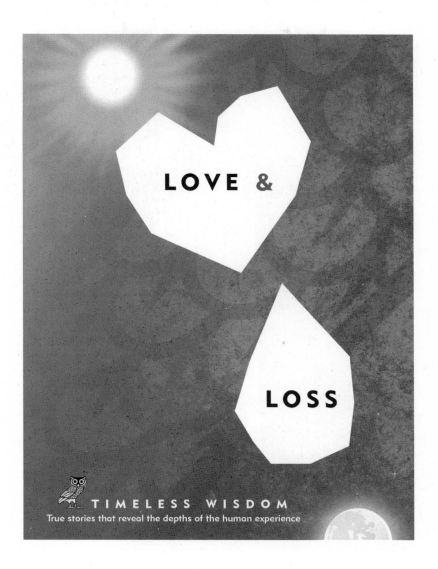

LOVE & LOSS

LOVE & LOSS

ISBN 978-1-925820-07-2

FEAR &

COURAGE

TIMELESS WISDOM
True stories that reveal the depths of the human experience

FEAR & COURAGE

ISBN 978-1-925820-06-5